PHILIPPIANS

Books by Gordon H. Clark

Readings in Ethics (1940)
Selections from Hellenistic Philosophy (1940)
A History of Philosophy (coauthor, 1941)
A Christian Philosophy of Education (1946, 1988)
A Christian View of Men and Things (1952, 1991)
What Presbyterians Believe (1956)[1]
Thales to Dewey (1957, 1989)
Dewey (1960)[2]
Religion, Reason and Revelation (1961, 1995)
William James (1963)[2]
Karl Barth's Theological Method (1963)
The Philosophy of Science and Belief in God (1964, 1987)
What Do Presbyterians Believe? (1965, 1985)
Peter Speaks Today (1967)[3]
The Philosophy of Gordon H. Clark (1968)
Biblical Predestination (1969)[4]
Historiography: Secular and Religious (1971, 1994)
II Peter (1972)[3]
The Johannine Logos (1972, 1989)
Three Types of Religious Philosophy (1973, 1989)
First Corinthians (1975, 1991)
Colossians (1979, 1989)
Predestination in the Old Testament (1979)[4]
I and II Peter (1980)[3]
Language and Theology (1980, 1993)
First John (1980, 1992)
God's Hammer: The Bible and Its Critics (1982, 1995)
Behaviorism and Christianity (1982)
Faith and Saving Faith (1983, 1990)
In Defense of Theology (1984)
The Pastoral Epistles (1984)
The Biblical Doctrine of Man (1984, 1992)
The Trinity (1985, 1990)
Logic (1985, 1988)
Ephesians (1985)
Clark Speaks From The Grave (1986)
Logical Criticisms of Textual Criticism (1986, 1990)
First and Second Thessalonians (1986)
Predestination (1987)
The Atonement (1987, 1996)
The Incarnation (1988)
Today's Evangelism: Counterfeit or Genuine? (1990)
Essays on Ethics and Politics (1992)
Sanctification (1992)
New Heavens, New Earth (1993)
The Holy Spirit (1993)
An Introduction to Christian Philosophy (1993)
Lord God of Truth (1994)
William James and John Dewey (1995)
God and Evil (1996)
Philippians (1996)

1. Revised as *What Do Presbyterians Believe?* (1965)
2. Combined as *William James and John Dewey* (1995)
3. Combined as *I & II Peter* (1980) and revised as *New Heavens, New Earth* (1993).
4. Combined as *Predestination* (1987).

PHILIPPIANS

GORDON H. CLARK

The Trinity Foundation

Philippians
Copyright ©1996 Lois A. Zeller and Elizabeth Clark George
Published by The Trinity Foundation
Hobbs, New Mexico 88240
ISBN:0-940931-47-8

Contents

Introduction vi
Preface vii
Chapter One 1
Chapter Two 45
Chapter Three 84
Chapter Four 106
Index 125
Scripture Index 135
The Crisis of Our Time 139
Intellectual Ammunition 145

INTRODUCTION

This commentary on Philippians is one of the last books that Gordon Clark wrote before his death in 1985; its date is about 1982. *Philippians* is the twelfth commentary Clark wrote–covering not quite half the New Testament corpus. It is, like his other commentaries, a concise and clear explanation of the meaning of the text. Clark makes it clear that Paul's letter is relevant to our situation at the end of the twentieth century. Paul may have written this letter nearly 2,000 years ago, but because it is the mind of God, it is normative for us today. Like all of God's Word, it is inerrant, necessary, comprehensible, and sufficient for our needs. May God grant the reader wisdom and understanding.

John W. Robbins
April 1996

PREFACE

Having published commentaries on several New Testament books, some characteristics of which have been misunderstood, I think a preliminary warning will help the readers of this commentary to understand its purpose more fully. First, the translation is not intended to be in the polished English style suitable for reading from the pulpit on Sunday morning. This translation is crabbed. It is so for two reasons. (A third might be that I am not competent enough to write in good style.) But the first is that Paul's Greek style is also crabbed, and I have tried to reproduce it as best as English can. Paul's sentences are often extremely complex, extremely long, and therefore involved. The Christians of Ephesus, Colosse, and Philippi must have had a hard time studying them. The modern reader also needs explanations. Some explanations can be made by breaking up Paul's sentences and making three or four out of one, but this is a form of explanation, and in my view it is better to show first what must be explained.

This leads to the second reason for the crabbed translation here imposed on an innocent public. It furnishes the reader of the modern polished versions with the best means of judging the merits of these several translations. With the King James, the Revised Standard Version, the New International Version, and the New American Standard before him, today's serious reader must often ask himself which version is correct, which one has altered the sense, what is the sense anyhow? A crabbed translation offers the best hope of being accurate. There may be mistakes in this present translation, but at least one source of error has been eliminated.

If an impatient reader cannot wait to determine the present author's evaluation of the versions, let it be said that the American Revised Version of 1901 or its later New American Standard edition is the most accurate of all. The King James is second in accuracy and first in style. The advertising campaigns of modern versions have unfairly maligned it. The Revised Standard Version makes some deliberate mistakes, more frequent in the Old Testament than in the New. The New International Version is too much of a paraphrase, but of course much better than the travesty of *Good News for Modern Man*. This should be sufficient to satisfy initial curiousity.

The main purpose, of course, which really underlies the preceding, is to explain the text. Some commentators, personally very devout, are so devotional that nothing is explained. The worst of these indulge in a saccharine sentimentality that tastes sour in the stomach. The best furnish light reading for light readers. Other authors, very liberal, are often so interested in undermining Biblical religion that their critical discussions crowd out the text, and again little or nothing is explained. Therefore this commentary ignores a whole section of modern scholarship and centers its attention on discovering precisely what Paul means. And that is what commentaries are supposed to do.

If then this commentary ignores some phases of New Testament scholarship–particularly the discussion of authenticity–the non-academic reader may wonder why in the world the much more technical, detailed, and dreary textual problems are introduced. Well, first, liberal destructive higher criticism has been completely defeated. There is probably not a single liberal critic in the whole world who dares to restrict Pauline authorship to Romans, 1 and 2 Corinthians, and Galatians, as they used to do. But the Westcott and Hort views on lower or textual criticism, once seemingly unquestioned, are now a matter of considerable discussion. Accordingly, if any ordinary American, who never hopes to become a professional scientist, is interested to learn that our spaceship to Saturn's rings devastated great areas of astronomy, so should any ordinary Christian take an interest in the less spectacular details of determining the text.

As the citizen knows no mathematics, so the ordinary Christian knows no Greek. But as the citizen reads that Saturn's rings are not rings at all, so too the Christian may be surprised to learn that there are several thousands of manuscripts of the New Testament (though only eighteen of Plato's *Timaeus,* and about seven of Aristotle's *Physics*); and they can hardly guess how many and how difficult textual problems are. This is precisely the reason why some examples are included here. With a little patience a person of ordinary intelligence can and ought to understand something of the issues involved. Just a little patience. Read slowly.

Readers may more justifiably regret the absence of historical detail. Some commentaries expound the passages in Acts which describe Paul's work in Philippi, plus some of the previous history of the city. Ralph Martin in *The Epistle of Paul to the Philippians* (Eerdmans, 1959), though his volume is small, gives thirty-five pages to a most interesting "Introduction." Perhaps instead of a long bibliography a few references to previous commentaries chosen at random would be welcome here. One of the very best is that of Lenski (Augsburg Publishing House, 1937). Hendriksen (Banner of Truth, 1963) is also excellent, except that he wanders too much into side issues and homiletic outlines. Of course the older nineteenth century commentaries, such as Eadie's (1859) are standard. H.C.G. Moule's (1897) is perhaps smaller, though the print is rather small so that its 116 pages may be equal to Eadie's 296. Jacobus J. Müller has one of 200 pages (Eerdmans, 1955). Merrill C. Tenney wrote a small book on *Philippians,* but it is not really a commentary. Also small but more of a commentary is Kenneth Grayston's contribution to the *Cambridge Bible Commentary on the New English Bible* (1967, 116 pages). Since there are also other commentaries, one may always doubt that another is needed. Obviously the present writer thinks he has a little something to add, and also something to subtract, but the reader must judge for himself.

Finally, not only must the paragraphs on textual criticism be read slowly, but nearly all the other paragraphs as well. It is essential that the reader keep his Bible open before him. Aside from some relaxing illustrative material, every line requires close attention to Paul's words. Be patient; study; meditate.

CHAPTER ONE

1:1, 2 Paul and Timothy, servants of Christ Jesus, to all the saints in Christ Jesus who are in Philippi with bishops and deacons: Grace to you and peace from God our Father and [the] Lord Jesus Christ.

Grayston, mentioned in the Preface, notes that Philippians is not a well organized letter. Chapter 1:1 to 3:1 goes smoothly, but then comes a "vigorous attack on opponents . . . with scarcely any warning." The original mood resumes at 4:2. Grayston outlines the critical view that because of this lack of over-all organization our present Philippians is the result of some scribe's combining three separate letters. He calls this hypothesis "persuasive as far as it goes," but questions any motivation for the scribe's combining the alleged separate letters. One who outlines books may use these divisions, if he wishes. H. C. G. Moule's commentary is only 116 pages long, and his comments are very short paragraphs on many of the Greek phrases–in fact, they are merely footnotes to the text. Instead of giving an outline, he summarizes the epistle in seven pages–longer than the epistle itself. No outline is given here, because outlines are to be made after one studies the epistle, not before.

The salutation is similar to those in the other Pauline epistles. In accordance with ancient custom, and some recent innovations in bureaucratic memos, the letter begins, rather than ends, with the writer's signature. In 2 Thessalonians 3:17 Paul says that he signed every epistle to support its authenticity. This seems to imply that Paul did not write Hebrews. One notes too that this letter comes from Paul and Timothy. Their names are joined, as is also the case in 1 and 2 Thessalonians, where Sylvanus is included. Timothy's name likewise appears in Philemon and Colossians. Personal affection, especially in the case of Timothy, and including Sylvanus' hard labor together in the cause of the Gospel, are a sufficient motivation. There is no need to infer that the language makes Timothy an apostle. Not even 2 Timothy 1:6, previously more fully explained in 1 Timothy 3:14, does this.

Though his name is joined to that of Paul in the greeting, the remainder is by Paul in the first person, with Timothy in the third person.

Paul and Timothy were both servants of Christ Jesus. The Greek word *douloi* actually means *slaves*. One may ask, How many Christians today think of themselves as slaves? Modern minds do not find slavery a comforting concept. The vicious atheist may say, "I am the Master of my fate, I am the Captain of my soul." Even if Christians find this a little too strong, they, especially the Arminians, show too much sympathy for the idea. If the apostles were slaves, must not we lesser Christians also be such? But this is a note missing in most pulpits. How many preachers ever refer to God as a *Despot*? But the New Testament, though not right here, uses that term.

However, although the Philippians were Greeks and were familiar with the horrors of Roman and even Greek slavery, Martin (55-56) thinks that Paul rather had in mind the *ebed Yahweh* of the Old Testament, a phrase used of Moses and the prophets. Nevertheless, *doulos* in the Gospels, including John, with hardly an exception, means servant or slave. Romans 6:16ff. very definitely means slaves. So also 1 Corinthians 7:2ff., and Colossians 3:22. This is not an exhaustive list, but it should be enough to prevent us from making the term *slave* too honorific, "a title of dignity" as Martin calls it (56). In Revelation 1:1 the term is applied to John and to some undesignated others. Revelation 2:20 and 7:3 apply it to Christians in general. Revelation 10:7 is restricted to the prophets. In 11:18 there are prophets and saints, both small and great. Revelation 15:3 refers to Moses alone. Revelation 19:2, 5 and 22:3, 6 refer to all. So much for the word *doulos.*

The addressees are all the saints in Philippi. This contrasts with the traditional position of Romanism, now somewhat modified, of restricting the use of the Bible to the priesthood and especially to the theologians. Even the priests know little about the Bible. A Roman Catholic sailor in the U.S. Navy came to a Protestant chaplain on one occasion–it was at the base in Albuquerque, and I know the chaplain well. In the conversation the chaplain pointed to some verse in Isaiah. Later the seaman reported the conversation to the Roman Catholic chaplain, who then called my friend. He asked, "You quoted something in Isaiah; is that in the Bible?" Having received the Protestant chaplain's assurance that it was, the Catholic chaplain then asked, "Is it in the Catholic Bible?" The answer seemed to satisfy him. Protestants recommend that all church members read the Bible, for Paul's letters are addressed to all.

With this true story about Romanism it is also pertinent to note that what the Roman church means by a *saint* is far removed from what the New Testament means. When the term *Holy* (*holy* and *saint* are the same word in Greek) is applied to God, it signifies his unique transcendence; when applied to human beings, it means that these persons are set apart for God's service. A Christian is of course obligated to obey the Ten Commandments, but the term *saint* does not designate any particular degree of actual sanctification.

Episcopoi and *diakonoi,* bishops and deacons, rather clearly designate officers of the church. The latter word can refer to any servant, but an *episcopos* is an *overseer.* Nevertheless even Anglican scholars admit that the New Testament term *episcopos* is more inclusive than their term *bishop.* One reason why Anglicans and Romanists cannot justify their form of ecclesiastical government, at least from this verse, is that here *episcopoi* is plural, and it is unlikely that there could have been two bishoprics in such a small city. The title simply refers to any elder. So too *diakonos* here can hardly refer to anyone else than a regularly installed church official.

Occasionally a commentator in his anti-Romish zeal, with which motivation I heartily agree, too greatly denigrates ecclesiastical offices. They may note, a little incorrectly, that Paul's main addressees are the people, and that the officers tag along after them. Eadie somehow stumbled onto the fact that Thomas Aquinas was embarrassed by this lack of respect for the bishop. To soften the apostle's language Aquinas wrote, "The apostle uses the order of nature, by which the flock usually preceded the shepherd. Here in processions the people come first and the priests and prelates follow." One gentleman points out, in reference to the relationship between people and officers, "The preposition is not 'under,' nor 'after,' but 'with' the bishops and deacons." This seems to presuppose that the previous word *saints* means the communicant members and that the officials are not included. Actually the phrase "all the saints" does not separate the addressees into two classes. The pastors and deacons are saints too. If we must stretch the Greek a little bit, it would be better to say, "all the saints, especially the overseers and deacons."

The benediction contains nothing unusual. With slight variations the benedictions in the other epistles all have essentially the same form.

1:3, 4 **I thank my God upon every [or, all] remembrance [or, mention] of you, always in every request of mine for you all, making my request with joy . . .**

The Preface of the present commentary mentioned others which do not much explain the meaning of the text. One example is *Philippian Studies* by J. A. Motyer. Perhaps he can excuse himself on the ground that he did not entitle his book a commentary. At any rate, a reader will see that his section on Philippians 1:3-7 (pages 16-22) does very little to explain what Paul wrote. For example, he says nothing about the possibilities indicated in the translation above.

One of the possibilities, but hardly even a possibility, is to take the pronoun "you" subjectively, that is, as the subject of a sentence: "you remember me"; instead of objectively, that is, "I remember you." A very few commentaries have been stupid enough to accept such an interpretation. It hardly needs discussion.

Two other interpretations are worthy of examination. Grayston follows the New English Bible's translation: "I thank my God whenever I think of you." Müller writes, "The thanksgiving is rendered 'upon all my remembrance of you,' i.e., 'every time I think of you' " (39, footnote). Ralph Martin says, "The preposition *upon*, *epi*, introduces the occasion of the thanksgiving, *upon every remembrance of you* [King James]. The Revised Version gives a more exact translation: 'upon all my remembrance of you,' suggesting the meaning that Paul renders thanks to God whenever he thinks of his Christian friends." Unfortunately the Revised Version's words and Martin's explanatory phrase do not mean precisely the same thing.

There is one difficulty that need not bother us. The word *mneia* can mean *remembrance* or *mention*. The word occurs seven times in the New Testament. In Romans 1:9, Ephesians 1:16, 1 Thessalonians 1:2, and 2 Timothy 3:6 the King James has *remembrance*. Grammarians maintain that *mneia* means *mention* only when the verb is *make:* to make mention of you. Otherwise it means *remembrance* as in the present instance. But in either case the same difficulty appears. The difficulty is this: Does Paul pray every time he remembers the Philippians or hears them mentioned? This is barely possible. He might remember when alone, and he would remember if someone mentions them; but there are too many situations in whch prayer is unlikely to follow. Suppose the jailer appears at that moment and roughly disturbs Paul's thoughts. A friend who mentions the Philippians to him might easily chatter rapidly along and Paul might listen to him instead of praying. One must notice too that these prayers of Paul were not simple prayers of thanksgiving. Even in the presence of the jailer or a talkative friend Paul might quickly and under his breath say, "Thank you, Lord." But the prayers the text describes included petitions. The term *dēesis* occurs twice. The word means a *request.* It is not likely that Paul would in every instance have time or opportunity to pray.

Eadie, whom so many later commentators fail to notice, gives a very plausible, an almost conclusive solution to this puzzle. To quote: "The phrase, *epi pasē tē mneia,* is not to be translated 'on every remembrance,' though such an interpretation is as old as Chrysostom . . . the article forbids it."

Tē is the article, *the,* attached to *mneia,* memory.

Eadie continues: "The meaning is not, 'as often as I remember . . .' but 'on my whole remembrance of you.' "

That is to say, Everything I remember about you leads me to thank God for you and to ask him to bless you in various ways.

Strange: So many later commentators pay no attention to something that must puzzle thousands of ordinary readers.

1:4 . . . because of your *koinonia* in the Gospel from the first day until now . . .

The matters of thanksgiving are more definitely specified than the petitions. Paul thanks God for the Philippians' *koinonia* in the Gospel. This Greek word is often translated *fellowship,* and a worse or more confusing translation can hardly be found. The American Standard Version has *participation,* and this is better. The Revised Standard Version and the New International Version have *partnership,* and this is probably the best, even though it does not quite express the meaning. *Koinonia* means "holding something in common." It can be a financial partnership where money and business interests are held in common; it can be the marriage relation; it can be the use of a common language. Anything held in common by two or more people is a *koinonia.* In this verse the common possession is explicitly said to be the Gospel. Paul and the Philippians both believed the same good news. It was the community or common agreement in theology that caused Paul to rejoice.

Commentators often say that this *koinonia* was not passive, but included an active furtherance of the Gospel. Hendriksen says it was "a fellowship in promoting the work of the Gospel . . . an active cooperation in Gospel activity" (52). This stretches the meaning of the preposition *eis* (*in* or *toward*) a little far. Lenski also holds that the *koinonia* is active, but his translation of *eis* is more restrained: "as regards the Gospel."

Although the verse itself barely suggests active promulgation of the Gospel, it is factually true that the Philippians actively participated or cooperated with Paul and his successors. Just how is not specified. Possibly they phoned their neighbors and offered to drive them to church the next Lord's Day morning. Later in the epistle (4:16) we learn that the Philippians on several occasions helped to support Paul with gifts of money. But the present verse cannot possibly be restricted to financial aid. In fact, supplying funds–certainly active cooperation–is hardly *koinonia,* for, as said above, *koinonia* means a common possession; and Paul did not possess the money until after it was sent, but after it was sent the Philippians did not possess it. Of course the Philippians were active in promulgating the Gospel. Of course they contributed funds. But these are not *koinonia.* What Paul and the Philippians held in common was the Gospel itself and the determination to make it known. Hence it seems that a very accurate translation of 1:4,5 could be, "making my petition with joy on the basis of our common possession with respect to the Gospel." In exegesis one must remember not to insert into the precise meaning of a verse additional ideas, even if those additions are expressed elsewhere. Then, too, the interpretation given here, which minimizes the idea of public activity, seems to receive support from the following context.

1:6 . . . being persuaded by this very thing, that

Philippians

he who has begun a good work in you will complete it until [the] day of Christ Jesus . . .

Before a more extensive explanation can be given, two grammatical points need to be decided. The first and more important concerns the reference to "this very thing." One possibility is: Because of the preceding verse, I am persuaded that Christ will continue his work in you. The translation would then be, "being persuaded by this very thing." The second possibility is: I am persuaded *of* this very thing; namely, that Christ will continue his work in you. The question is: Does "this very thing" refer to what precedes or to what follows? Some expositors, Lenski for example, argue that "*Perithō* does not govern the accusative" (709), but strangely his interpretation makes it do so: "this very thing, namely that . . . ." Hendriksen apparently agrees (54, note 32), for he explicitly uses the term "namely." But he pays much less attention to the problem than does Lenski. Müller writes, "particular stress is laid on *auto touto*. The accusative after *pepoithōs* is unusual–the verb being usually followed by a preposition–but the same construction is found again in verse 25. A fuller description of *auto touto* follows after it, introduced by *hoti*" (41). Indeed, verse 25 has the same construction, but it does not present the same puzzle. Eadie also asserts that the verb, "though it often takes the genitive, here governs the accusative" (11). Actually the verb usually takes the dative, when the object is a noun rather than a clause. (See Blass and Debrunner, 187, 6.) When it is a clause, it may be introduced by *hoti* or *hina* (that). A reader of a commentary may be repelled by these (insufficient) details of Greek grammar; but they illustrate to him how many problems an exegete has to consider. No intelligent choice can be made without a knowledge of the possibilities.

However, there is another consideration. Although one should never violate the grammar, the grammar may allow for possibilities that only the context can decide. The interpretation that "this very thing" refers to the following clause gives no reason why

Paul was persuaded. The words suddenly appear from nowhere. Hence I think it better to say, "Because of your interest in the Gospel over this substantial period of time, I am persuaded that . . . ." This makes much better sense.

The second grammatical problem in this verse is both easier to solve and more closely connected with the interesting main thought. It has to do with the reference to "the day of Christ."

In contrast with all the other versions I have seen, the Revised Standard Version has, "will bring it to completion at the day of Jesus Christ." This allows and even suggests the possibility that Christ does nothing for us in the meantime. Such an interpretation is impossible theology, and, if the patient reader will permit it, apparently impossible Greek as well. The preposition *achri* occurred just two lines above in the phrase "until the present." The cooperation of the Philippians in the Gospel continued from the first day until now. It is nonsense to say that they cooperated from the first day *at* the present moment. Some instances of the preposition are: Matthew 24:38, "eating and drinking, marrying and giving in marriage *until* the day that Noe entered into the ark." Compare Luke 17:27. Luke 1:20: "Thou shalt be dumb and not able to speak until the day that these things shall be performed." Luke 21:24: "Jerusalem shall be trodden down of the Gentiles until the times of the Gentiles be fulfilled." See also Acts 1:2, 2:29, 3:21, 7:18, 23:1. The difficult language of 2 Corinthians 10:13, 14 is also inconsistent with the meaning of *at,* either in time or space. Those who wish may check the remainder of the forty-nine instances of *achri.* The idea that Christ, or anyone else, will wait to complete something on a given day makes perfectly good sense in itself. But it does not fit this context.

A few paragraphs above, some mention was made of the Philippians' active participation in the proclamation of the Gospel. The comment was that the verse did not refer to any overt activity because such activity would not be a common possession. Here we come closer to such activity. Müller makes a good point when he says, " 'A good work' undoubtedly [at least presumably] has a wider meaning than the previously mentioned partnership in the Gospel and denotes a more comprehensive work of grace in the hearts of believers both in inward disposition and the outward activity." Although it is still called the work of Christ, the time span from the initiation to the day of Jesus Christ strongly suggests some sort of activity by the Philippians themselves. With some intermediate hints, the climax is found in 2:12.

We come now to the very important pronouncement that Christ who began [this] good work in you will complete it–carry it on to completion–until [the] day of Christ Jesus. Important though it be, Lenski, who is usually so detailed, has little to say about it–perhaps because he is a Lutheran and not a Calvinist. Hendriksen, surely a Calvinist with a name spelled like that, uses up a bit more than two pages in trivialities.

This great verse is one of the great verses supporting the Calvinistic doctrine of the perseverance of the saints, which doctrine Arminians condemned as one of the five essential and essentially false doctrines of Calvinism. But how can anyone eradicate the idea from this great verse? Christ will complete the work he began. As Neander said, "Gottes Art ist ja nicht, etwas halb zu thun."

This then is the first point: The work of salvation in the heart or soul was initiated by Christ, not by the human person. The text does not say that because Christ began to work after the sinner had started the good work, he, Christ, would continue his efforts too. The text says that Christ began the good work. He also will perfect or complete it, continuing his work throughout the now regenerated sinner's life.

One commentator, who somewhat grudgingly admits that this is so, hurries on to insist that nonetheless the regenerated soul, the saint, is not passive, but himself does a lot of work, too. This sort of statement needs to be examined for accuracy, distinctions, and exaggerations. In the first place, as already said, the sinner does not initiate the good work. As the Westminster Confession says, the sinner is "made willing by his grace"; and "this effectual call is of God . . . and not from anything at all foreseen in man, who is altogether passive therein" (X, 1 and 2). Human depravity is so all inclusive (VI, 1-6) that "a natural man, being altogether averse from that [spiritual] good, and dead in sin, is not able by his own strength to convert himself or to prepare himself thereunto" (IX, 4).

But so anxious are many people to find some trace of initiative and merit in man that after they briefly mention the work of God, they expatiate on the work of man. In one way or another they side-step or obscure the main point. For example, Motyer says that "Paul *saw in the Philippians* [ital. added] the feature of *perseverance* [ital. his] in that they had prolonged their fellowship 'from the first day until now' (verse 5) and *endurance* [ital. his] ..." (21).

It is clearly false that Paul could see in their conduct that they would persevere. Some apparently sincere converts did not persevere–Demos for instance. Paul's statement is not a deduction from empirical observation, but a revelation from God. Eadie rightly observes, "The apostle's confidence ... rested on his knowledge of God's character and methods of operation ..." (12). A few lines below he rejects the perversion: "He among you who has begun a good work will continue to do well until death." Such violent mistranslations show to what lengths some Arminians will go.

Of course the Philippians not only believed the Gospel, they also cooperated with Paul by overt action. It is true that after regeneration, but only after regeneration, a saint can actively accomplish a modicum of spiritual good. Yet even his actions, as Paul will later indicate in 2:13, are God's works. The perfecting process, which Christ initiated, is also controlled throughout by God's working in us.

It is because of this that we may know that every regenerate person will persevere to the end. Did we in our own strength confide, our striving would be losing.

We have been talking about the perseverance of the saints until the day of their death. But, though it may seem strange, the verse says more. Christ continues the good work in us until the day of his return. Now, the Shorter Catechism says, "The souls of believers are at their death made perfect in holiness, and do immediately pass into glory; and their bodies, being still united to Christ, do rest in their graves till the resurrection." True, of course. But the present verse adds something: Christ continues the good work in us until he returns. It seems that though we are made perfect in holiness at our death, Christ's blessings to us continue to multiply even in Heaven.

Because of the pervasive Arminianism among the relatively evangelical Christian groups in America today, a short historical note will help to show the importance of this doctrine. During the Reformation period of the sixteenth century the anti-Romish movement was unfortunately divided into Lutherans and Calvinists. Had Luther's successor been someone other than Melanchthon this rift might have been closed. Early in the seventeenth century within the Calvinistic movement, Arminians revolted and retreated, not all the way, but a few steps back toward the Romish theology. In Switzerland, Holland, Great Britain, and even in Ireland Reformed confessions were formulated. These culminated in the Westminster Confession just before the mid-century mark. This Confession, and its accompanying two catechisms, in agreement with the Swiss and Belgic confessions, expressed what the English-speaking Protestants regarded as the central doctrines of the Bible. It was to have been the unifying position in the British Isles. But the English throne went to a secret Catholic, then to an open Catholic, and the hopes of the English Puritans and Scottish Presbyterians were cruelly suppressed. A few lines from this last and greatest Reformed confession are now to be quoted with several paragraphs from the present writer's *What Do Presbyterians Believe?*

The Westminster Confession, chapter XVII, says:

> They whom God hath accepted . . . can neither totally nor finally fall away from the state of grace; but shall certainly persevere therein to the end and be eternally saved. This

perseverance of the saints depends not upon their own free will, but upon the immutability of the decree of election. . . .

Here now are a few paragraphs from my previous publication.

One evening as I was conducting the mid-week prayer meeting, an elderly, white-haired gentleman asked for one of his favorite hymns: "How Firm a Foundation." The hymn has six long stanzas, and as the meeting was very informal I wondered aloud which of the six we could omit. Not the first, of course–it speaks of the Word of God as the foundation of our faith; not the second because we need the aid and strength of God's omnipotent hand; the third or fourth? The old gentleman interrupted my wondering by insisting that this was a good hymn and that we could sing it all. We did, and as we reached the fifth stanza, everyone else in the room saw in it the picture of the grand old man who had requested the hymn:

E'en down to old age all my people shall prove
My sovereign, eternal, unchangeable love.
And when hoary hairs shall their temples adorn,
Like lambs they shall still in my bosom be borne.

He too sang it with vigor, and he sang the sixth stanza too:

The soul that on Jesus hath leaned for repose
I will not, I will not desert to his foes.

Now it was a bit strange that this gentleman should have requested this hymn and should have sung it with such praise and devotion. For he did not like Calvinism; all his life he had been an Arminian; he did not believe in "eternal security," as he called it; and he had been telling his friends so for years. Even now he would have disowned the name of Calvinism. But could it be that without realizing it he had now come to believe, and that his earlier Arminian views had changed with the color of his hair?

If it is strange that this lovely Arminian saint could become at least somewhat of a Calvinist without knowing it, it is far more strange that anyone who bases his faith on the firm foundation of God's Word could ever be an Arminian. The Scripture verses are too numerous to mention.

But some may be puzzled at the doctrine of perseverance and think that it ascribes too much will power to frail humanity. Such an objection rests on a misunderstanding. Section ii of this chapter clearly says that "this perseverance of the saints depends not upon their own free will, but upon the immutability of the decree of election." I remember a conversation with another Arminian. He had been fulminating against the doctrine of election and I replied that election was the basis of our assurance of salvation. The Arminian's contempt rose in his face as he charged me with substituting the doctrine of election for the crucifixion of Christ. Well of course, our salvation is based on the active and passive obedience of Christ; but our assurance requires some reason to believe that the benefits of Christ's work are permanantly applied to ourselves. Small comfort it is indeed if we are saved at breakfast and lost at noon. Let us emphasize the fact: The Arminians can have no sure hope of entering Heaven. They must always entertain the uncomfortable feeling that they will finally be lost. Obviously no man can depend on his own power to persevere in grace; for, first, human nature is weak, and, second, grace is not something we can earn or keep. And if the Arminian refuses to admit that God causes his elect to persevere, what reasonable expectation can he have of Heaven?

The Roman Catholic doctrine, to which the Arminians reverted in their revolt against the Reformation, is expressed in the decrees of the Council of Trent. One section reads, "If anyone maintain that a man once justified cannot lose grace, . . . let him be accursed." Only a massive ignorance of the Scriptures allows for such a position.

If Philippians 1:6 is as clear as it is possible for language to be, John 10:28-29 are still clearer: "And I give unto them eternal life; and they shall never perish, neither shall any man pluck them out of my hand. My Father, which gave them me, is greater than all; and no man is able to pluck them out of the Father's hand."

How some people have squirmed to avoid these verses. Those who insist on a free will independent of God say that although other men cannot pluck a child of God from the Father's hand, the man himself is free to do so. But the verse says no man can do so: This includes the man himself. Another act of desperation is to argue that although no man can pluck the child from the hand of God, the devil can do so. But once more, the phrase no man in the King James Version is in the original "no one." So it is translated in the American Revised Version. And in any case the verse says that Christ gives his sheep eternal life. Would it be eternal if it ceased after five days or five years? The verse also says that they shall never perish. How long and how sure is never? It would seem that no one could misunderstand this language.

Then for good measure we shall add 1 Peter 1:5, which speaks of the regenerate as those "who are kept by the power of God through faith unto salvation ready to be revealed in the last time." Why belabor the obvious? And still the Scriptures, addressed as they are to stubborn rebels against God, repeat the same idea time after time. Compare 2 Timothy 2:19; Jeremiah 31:3, and 32:40; 1 John 2:19; and Isaiah 55:11.

Of course, the perseverance of the saints does not mean sinless perfection or a life free from struggle and temptation. Eradication of our corrupt nature is a long and difficult process and will not be completed until we are glorified. As long as the present life continues, we may become careless of the means of grace, our hearts may be temporarily hardened, we may fall into grievous sins. Thus we may harm others and bring temporal punishment upon ourselves. God does not promise to carry us to the skies on flowery beds of ease. But praise his name, he promises to carry, drag, or push us there. So, and only so, we arrive. What should be particularly noted in this section is how the doctrine of perseverance fits in with all the other doctrines. God is not irrational or insane. What he says hangs together; it forms a logical system. Election, total depravity, effectual calling, sovereign grace, and perseverance are mutually consistent. God does not contradict himself. But Arminian saints do. They may be grand old men, loved by all who know them. But not until the message of the Bible persuades them of God's sovereign, unchangeable love, can they really sing,

The soul, though all Hell should endeavor to shake,
I'll never, no, never, no never forsake.

Because of the great importance of the subject, this has been a long exposition for a single verse. Even so, a footnote seems to be in order. It is this: The subject has been *perseverance,* not *assurance* of salvation. Like any other two topics in theology, they are related, and much more closely related than some other pairs. Yet assurance and perseverance are not the same thing. Arminians, at least some I have met, assert assurance but deny perseverance. One one occasion a very Arminian college invited me to give a lecture on philosophy. The lecture stayed within the bounds of the advertised topic. But afterward the head of the Philosophy Department took me to lunch and we talked about assurance. He assured me that he was assured of his salvation. I am sure, he said, that if I should die right now, I would go to Heaven. But as I tried gently to tell him, he was not assured that if he did not die until the following week he would get to Heaven. He might "fall from grace" in the interval.

Note that being assured of salvation does not mean that one will be saved. Aside from Arminians there was the Catholic plumber who was sure the Church would get him past the pearly gates. Many people are assured that God is too good to punish anybody. Others are assured of many things that are not so–for example, that a forked branch can point out a good place to dig a well. Assurance may be a delusion, but the perseverance of the saints is God's truth.

1:7 **... just as it is right for me to think this for all of you because I hold you in my heart, for both in my chains and in my defense and certification of the Gospel you all are sharers with me in the grace.**

This is a difficult verse both to translate and to explain. First, there are two grammatical or linguistic problems. Of these two one is the word *just* or *right.* The Greek word is *dikaion* and it means justice. *Justification* and *righteousness* are derived from it. It is a little strange to say that Paul's thinking of the Philippians was a judicial matter. Grayston remarks, "It is not easy to be sure of the exact meaning of this verse. The Greek is in part ambiguous and, instead of 'It is indeed only right ...' [New English Bible], could be translated: 'I am justified in taking this view about you all ...'." Lenski says, " 'Meet for me' (Authorized Version) is incorrect; 'right for me' (Revised Version) is correct, it would be wrong, *adikon,* if Paul were minded otherwise. 'To think this of you all' (Authorized Version) is likewise incorrect, [but] 'on behalf of them all' " (711).

The second linguistic problem is easily solved. The King James is clearly wrong in saying "partakers of my grace." Its margin is correct: "partakers with me of grace." The New English Bible is very poor because it substitutes the less definite word *privilege* for the more definite *grace.*

There is a third difficulty, well, hardly a difficult difficulty, which combines linguistics and interpretation. As many as four– incredible!–four commentators read, "Because you have me in your heart." Grammatically of course this is unimpeachable. But it is equally grammatical, and also required by the context, to read "because I have you in my heart."

Beyond grammar the difficulties are historical. His bonds surely refer to his being chained in prison, indicating that the government had curtailed his earlier relative freedom. But *apologia* and especially *bebaiōsei* (apology and certification or confirmation) could be taken more broadly. Of course *apologia* rather definitely means a defense in court. Remember the Platonic dialogue *The Apology of Socrates*. Nevertheless, 1 Peter 3:14 cannot possibly be restricted to court cases. *Bebaiōsis* is even more easily extended. The Greek *te-kai* (both-and), indicating some difference between the bonds and the *apologia-bebaiōsis,* also prevent us from definitely restricting the meaning to the prison and court. One can imagine, though of course it is only a supposition, that the three words describe a progression: chains in jail, argument in court and elsewhere, certification or confirmation in all his preaching. Lenski disagrees: "Since it *[apologia]* is here combined under one article with *bebaiosis,* another term with a reference to a court in this combination, we are sure that Paul is referring to his trial (713). Although I am not so sure of this, yet Lenski continues with an important observation: "Note the difference: 'my bonds' but not 'my defense.' It is the defense and confirmation of a far greater defendant, namely, 'of the Gospel.' The fate of his person was of the least concern to Paul, the fate of the Gospel was everything" (713).

The final phrase of the verse is also difficult. Several commentators make no reference to it. Moule makes it a dangling clause, the *you* just before the last word of the verse repeating the *you* two lines above in "having *you* in my heart." Thus the translation would be "you all being copartners." Moule continues, "copartners of my grace"; but "my copartners of grace" seems better. Lenski agrees, referring also to verse three.

1:8 **For God is my witness, how I long for you all in the affection of Christ Jesus.**

It is surprising how many commentators have massacred this verse, due of course to the offensive word *splagchnois*. The ancients had a lively connection between psychology and physiology. For Plato, dreams occurred on the surface of the liver. Today, contrary to Biblical usage, the heart is made to mean the emotions. Here Paul's affections are his innards, entrails, his lungs, liver, kidneys, or in the case of a woman, her womb. Acts 1:18 uses the word in the case of Judas, when he fell headlong and all his guts gushed out.

Of course the Bible does not place God's stamp of approval on the ancient psychology. The terminology, though sometimes literal, had become a customary metaphor, just as we do not really mean that emotions and thoughts are the motions of the heart as it pumps the blood. The physiological psychology is gone; the metaphor remains.

One may note that this verse is given as a reason for the preceding verse: It is right for me to think of you, and God is my witness that I do so. It is somewhat strange that Paul calls upon God as his witness. Of course, this is not profanity; it is solemnity. But was Paul so fearful that the Philippians would doubt his interest in them that he had to call upon God? Motyer on 1:8-11 (23-30) is oblivious of the question. Grayston says nothing at all on 1:8. Moule briefly suggests that Paul was "tried by unkind suspicions." Tenney refers to the verse in three places but has nothing on this question. Lenski, Hendriksen, Müller, and Martin only note Paul's earnestness.

But if we do not know Paul's motivation, how can we obey his admonition to imitate him and call God as our witness on occasion? When Christ was on trial, he swore a legal oath. Then we may do the same. But surely, if it is not profanity, it is at least irreverent to call upon God's name in every trivial circumstance. Remember that James said, "Swear not at all, neither by Heaven, neither by the Earth, neither by any other oath; but let your yea be yea and your nay nay, lest you fall into condemnation." Does James contradict Christ and does Paul leave us in the lurch? Or is there a promise later in 3:15 that our perplexity will be removed?

1:9 **And this I pray, that your love abound more and more in knowledge and every sensation . . .**

It is possible, quite grammatically, to translate the verse as "I pray that your love abound by means of knowledge." Eadie quotes one commentator who so understands the verse, though he himself rejects this interpretation. But the Greek proposition *en* means *by* about as often as it means *in*. Müller seems to agree: "that their love may abound more and more with knowledge . . . in advanced knowledge" (45). His footnote, however, is more than doubtful: "*epignōsis* is a stronger word than *gnōsis*." In the later Hellenistic Greek of the New Testament the prefixed preposition has lost any separate force it may have had in the classical language. Lenski is also mistaken and he is even worse in saying, "Paul often uses the word in the sense of knowledge of the heart and not mere knowledge of the head" (718). This is unscriptural. Nowhere in the Bible is a distinction made between the head and the heart. The Biblical distinction is between the heart and the lips. "With their lips do [they] honor me but . . . their heart [is] far from me" (Isaiah 29:13).

The modern romantic temperament regards love as an emotion, with the heart as its organ. But in Scripture the heart thinks and plans. Christian love is not an emotion, but a volition. Such was the common view of the church until relatively recently, but people today are more influenced by Freud than by Augustine. One reason for insisting that Christian love is a volition is that God commands love. Emotions cannot be commanded. Even a fickle college student, girl or boy, if the two are in love, could hardly obey a command to love someone else. Emotions cannot be commanded. Volitions can.

Furthermore the connection between love and knowledge is much closer than most present day Christians imagine. The New

Chapter One

Testament defines love as obedience to the law (Romans 13:10; 1 John 2:5; 5:2,3); but voluntary obedience presupposes a previous understanding and knowledge. For this reason Ellicott is mistaken when he says, "nor, lastly, is *en* here instrumental, as love could hardly be said to increase by the agency of knowledge" (27).

The text's wording at this point is somewhat peculiar. The King James' *judgment* (margin, *sense*), New American Standard *discernment,* and New International Version's *depth of insight,* are used to translate *aisthēsis, sensation.* This is the only case of *aisthēses* in the New Testament, though the verb *aisthanomai* is found in Luke 9:45, and *aistheterion* occurs in Hebrews 5:14. In Luke the verb must mean *to understand.* In Hebrews the King James version and the New American Standard have *senses,* but since it cannot possibly mean *senses,* the Revised Standard Version has *faculties* (a sort of cop-out); and the New International Version has the surprising word *themselves.* In classical Greek the verb can mean perception or taking note of, though the noun usually, but not always, is restricted to sensation. That the wider Hellenistic meaning is correct here is evident both from the immediately preceding mention of knowledge and the immediately succeeding reference to moral judgments. No one could ever *sense* right or wrong.

Motyer's *Philippian Studies,* though not usually serving as a commentary, as indicated earlier, has some remarks worth quoting on the present point.

> We [in modern times] would not have immediately associated love and knowledge, but the connection is readily understandable if we take a concordance to the word here translated "knowledge." It occurs twenty times in the New Testament and always with exclusive reference to knowledge of the things of God, religious knowledge, spiritual knowledge, theological knowledge (cf. Rom. 1:28, RV; Col. 2:2). . . . Truth is an essential ingredient in Christian experi-

ence. To be a Christian, a man must come to know the truth. To continue and to grow as a Christian a man must increasingly grasp the truth, learning it in depth as well as in breadth. ... Ignorance is a root cause of stunted growth among Christians (27-28).

Motyer does not put the matter too strongly.

1:10 ... so that you may [be able to] evaluate things that differ, in order that you may be genuine and blameless until the day of Christ ...

Here it is clear that Paul has intellectual judgment in mind, not sensation. It is a matter of evaluation. The phrase "things that differ" is sometimes paraphrased by "approve things that are excellent," as the King James has it. This obscures the evaluating or estimating included in the verb *dokimadzein*. Paul very definitely has in mind the comparison, discrimination, and judging between goods and evils. Hendriksen tries to avoid this translation by referrring to 4:8,9; but his argument is a fallacy. Those verses simply tell us to think about what is good. But this does not deny, it even presupposes, that one must first discriminate between things that differ. Moule and Eadie agree.

The purpose of this intellectual judgment is that the Christian should be genuine, sincere, pure, or some such word, and void of offense. This last word *(aproskopoi)* permits two interpretations. It can refer to the commission of an offense against the law, or it can refer to actions that cause other people to stumble and sin. In view of the previous idea of discrimination and judgment, it seems better to understand Paul as urging the Philippians themselves to avoid sinful actions. If the first term, *sincere,* refers to a subjective state, the second term most likely does so also. Once again, this does not mean that a Christian is free to cause others to stumble. It simply means that the present verse envisages the

Philippians' own character. It seems to me that the following verse supports this interpretation.

1:11 ... being filled with the fruit of righteousness which is through Jesus Christ to the glory and praise of God.

The first phrase, "being filled with the fruit of righteousness" surely refers to the character of the Philippian Christians. That some of this is connected with his concern for others is not to be denied, but the main idea is entirely subjective. Indeed the next phrase, "through Jesus Christ," enforces this view. The sanctification of the Christian is controlled by him who began the good work.

Martin (66-67) stresses this individualistic interpretation somewhat more than is warranted. Taking a hint from the word *fruit* in the singular, he wants it to refer to one thing only: justification, the possession of Christ's righteousness by faith. Or, if not strictly "one thing only," then "the evidence of such right relationship in the display of those characteristics which are described in Galatians v. 22. . . . The following clause 'which are by Jesus Christ' would lend support to the first interpretation in the light of Paul's doctrine of justification by faith in Christ." I do not think so, for the work of Christ which is envisaged in 1:5-11 is a work now going on, not an instantaneous judicial decision of acquittal.

The final phrase of the verse is "to the glory and praise of God." This last phrase hardly needs, hardly allows, any explanation. Most commentators make one or two otiose remarks and let it go at that. More profitable perhaps for modern readers might be a contrast between Christian ethics and the theory of John Dewey. He holds that all action, or all good action, is purposive. Men invent light bulbs in order to see better. They want to see better in order to read the stock market reports more accurately, the purpose of which is to increase their assets, which of course enables them to buy a car, so they can drive to Yosemite, and–here is the point–

and so on forever. There is no end. Value consists only in efficiency toward a goal, which in itself has no value, but is valuable only because it leads to something else equally valueless in itself. One can reasonably criticize Dewey, and most secular theories of ethics, by pointing out that this make life meaningless. Such theories cannot show that continuing to live is better than suicide. In debates with the secularists, this point is, I believe, very effective. But for the moment and for this final phrase of the verse, its support of the first question of the Shorter Catechism is important. "What is the chief end of man? Man's chief end is to glorify God and to enjoy him forever." Buying a car, and driving either to church or to Yosemite, is to glorify God. Secularists of course will not admit that this end is worthwhile; but at any rate Christian ethical theory provides a final end without which nothing is worth anything.

Verse 11 seems to end a section of the epistle and could be used in outlining a summary. The first comment of this commentary is that outlines and summaries should be made, if at all, after studying the epistle, not before. Hendriksen does this. He starts a summary on page 63. But its usefulness is problematic. It adds nothing and subtracts a good deal. A thought that is omitted in a summary might be of great importance in a given situation and rather irrelevant in another. For "guidance," which so many Christians woefully misunderstand, the best procedure is to study all the Scripture, remember as much as possible, and then hope that what is pertinent to a present personal difficulty will come to mind when needed. The idea of waiting for trouble to arise, and then beginning to search the Scriptures, is a poor method. Of course it is worse to wait for "the leading of the Spirit" without the knowlege, discrimination, and judgment that honest intellectual study alone will bring.

Although nearly all manuscripts read "praise of God," and only about half a dozen have either *Christ* or *him*, Aland's 1966 edition gives this almost unanimous reading only a C rating, though Metzger allows it a B rating. Why not an A rating, since Metzger himself says, "there is little doubt that the original reading is *kai epainon theou*"?

Textual criticism is a queer science. One of its rules is that the more difficult reading is to be preferred. Now, in addition to *Christ*, a reading *me* (to *my* praise) occurs in two Greek and one Latin manscripts. This reading is so difficult that it is quite impossible. Should it therefore be preferred as absolutely certain? The reason for the rule is that a scribe, when he does not understand the text, will substitute something superficially easier. No doubt this is sometimes the case; but an inadvertent mistake, when the scribe's eyes are growing fuzzy, can also produce a reading more difficult than the original.

1:12, 13, 14 **I want you to know, brethren, that my affairs have rather resulted in** [a rather unusual meaning for this verb] **the advance of the Gospel. So that my imprisonment has become evident in Christ in the whole Praetorium and to all the others, and most of the brethren in the Lord are persuaded by my bonds [imprisonment] more zealously to dare to speak the word without fear.**

Various commentators have made it clear that Paul was more interested in the advance of the Gospel than in his own safety. The Philippians were concerned over both points, and Paul assures them that the circumstances of his imprisonment had resulted in a wider proclamation and acceptance of the Gospel than might otherwise have occurred.

The *Praetorium* was not Caesar's palace, as the King James has it, nor exactly the barracks of the Praetorian Guard. It probably refers to the soldiers themselves, whose duty it was to guard the prisoners. the phrase "all the others" seems to refer to other people, soldiers or civilians, who had some undefined function in the judicial system. Since Paul's imprisonment lasted for two years or so, and since the Praetorium was a body of 9,000 men, Paul had reason to be glad that so many heard the Gospel. Indeed, all the others could mean the inhabitants of Rome in general. In 1:13 the words "my bonds became evident in Christ" hint at an important fact. Most probably they mean that the soldiers had learned the charges made against Paul, that these charges were not the usual charges of crime or treason, but were strictly religious. Though not its literal translation the verse can be paraphrased as "it became evident to all the guardsmen that my imprisonment was due to my preaching Christ." This would be a *cause célèbre,* and one can imagine that the soldiers would discuss it among themselves.

Yet this much is not all that relates to the promulgation of the Gospel. Paul's conduct was so remarkable that it encouraged the Christians in Rome, who presumably had been somewhat fearful, to proclaim the Gospel publicly and with boldness. It is interesting to note that Paul did not say "many" of the brethren spoke boldly, but "most" did.

The critical edition has "to speak the word." Some of the most ancient manuscripts have "to speak the word of God." The textual critics give their shorter reading a D rating; and this seems the part of wisdom.

1:15   Some even through envy and contention, but others through good will, are preaching Christ...

The promulgation of the Gospel in Rome was not without some unfortunate aspects. The psychology of preaching the Gospel because of envy and for the purpose of contention is hard to understand. A popular evangelist today may be envious of the greater success another more popular evangelist has had. But envy can hardly be his motivation. If one of these preaches fundamental heresy, contention may be justified. But this verse gives no indication that the preaching mutilated or destroyed the Gospel. Therefore, although Paul does not give us the needed information, it seems likely that these envious and contentious preachers were not Judaizers. The Judaizers actually demolished the Gospel because, even though they claimed to trust Christ for salvation, they trusted the food laws in addition. In Galatia this called forth Paul's vigorous denunciation. Here he does not curse the preachers, but takes pleasure in their preaching. Moule's identification therefore must be incorrect (20). Neither is Tenney on the right track. He says that "disloyal preachers with selfish motives were trying to tear Paul's work apart." This is a little ambiguous. Maybe these envious preachers were trying to tear Paul apart, and therefore in a sense could be said to be tearing Paul's work apart; but Paul does not say they preach "another gospel." He approves the contents of their sermons. Verse 15 at least hints that the contentious and the sincere both preach Christ. This was not so in the case of the Judaizers.

> **1:16, 17, 18 . . . the latter out of love, knowing that I am set for the defense of the Gospel; the former preach Christ out of strife, not from pure motives, thinking to raise up tribulation in my chains. But what of it? Except that in every way, whether in pretense or in truth [sincerity?] Christ is proclaimed, and in this I rejoice; indeed I shall [continue to] rejoice . . .**

Eadie waxes verbose on this passage for a full eleven pages. There is no explicable difficulty here that requires such a lengthy exposition. There is perhaps an inexplicable difficulty, which we can only note and pass on.

Verse 16 continues the sentence in verse 15. Those who had been emboldened to preach publicly were divided into two groups. Some preached from good motives; some did not. The former loved both Paul and the Gospel. They knew and were inspired by the fact that Paul was completely devoted to the defense of the Gospel.

The word for defense is *apologia:* in technical theology, *apologetics.* Some misguided Christians today repudiate argumentation. The New Testament does not. Not only is *apologia* in 1 Peter 3:15; it is also in Acts 22:1, 1 Corinthians 9:3, 2 Corinthians 7:11, and Philippians 1:7, as we recently saw. Mark 9:10 has the disciples "questioning one with another" *(suzēteō)*–they were acting properly. In Mark 12:28 a scribe had heard Jesus arguing with the Sadducees. Acts 6:9 has some people disputing with Stephen and clearly Stephen disputed with them, as 6:10 very forcefully indicates. Barnabas in Acts 9:29 defends the recently converted Paul by telling the suspicious disciples that Paul disputed against the Grecians. Well, these verses should be enough to silence those who think that a Christian should not argue.

The inexplicable difficulty is the psychology of those who preached Christ in order to cause trouble for Paul. The words of the text are easy to understand; the motivation is not. Most commentators point out that these enemies of Paul were not Judaizers. Their preaching was orthodox and Paul not only approved of it but rejoiced in it. Paul did not approve the preaching of the Judaizers. He condemned it and them in the harshest terms. Here the sin was not heresy but insincerity or evil motives. But this is hard to understand. If they wished to distress Paul, they could have better succeeded by attacking his doctrine. They must have been somewhat stupid.

There is also another puzzle, though it is more easily solved. How could Paul rejoice at this insincere preaching? Can God convert peole through the work of evil evangelists? Is someone in Heaven today because he heard the preaching of Judas Iscariot a few months before the betrayal? The answer is that God can, and maybe Judas saved someone. The reason is that a man is justified by believing certain doctrines. It makes no difference from whom he heard the good news. If he believes the information he is thereby justified. Naturally this does not excuse the insincerity of the preacher. Fortunately a sinner's salvation does not depend on the character of the preacher–it depends upon the sinner's believing the message.

There is a story that I have some reason to believe is true. In the University of Pennsylvania a professor of history read to his class Jonathan Edwards' sermon "Sinners in the Hands of an Angry God." The aim of the professor was to show how harsh, disagreeable, and morose the New England Puritans were. Because of this reading, however, at least one student was converted to Christianity.

One minor point: How did these enemies of Paul expect to add to his tribulations as the King James translates it? The New International Version has a better translation: to "stir up trouble for me while I am in chains." But what were the tribulations? Moule suggests that the tribulation would consist in the attempts and the expected success in preventing converts from visiting Paul in jail. Paul would thus not only enjoy less company, he would be prevented from giving these new Christians some additional instruction for their growth in grace. But is this severe enough to provoke Paul's remark?

1:19, 20 **... for I know that for me this will result toward salvation through your prayer and supply of the spirit of Jesus Christ, according to the earnest expectation and my hope that in nothing shall I be ashamed, but in all boldness as always also now Christ shall be magnified in my body, whether through life or through death.**

These are verses of some difficulty. Look at the word *salvation*. Paul in the assurance of his eternal salvation would hardly say that he will enter Heaven because of his imprisonment and the Philippians' prayer. Of course he might say that his execution would usher him into Heaven, but the latter part of the verse does not predict his execution–it is merely possible. Then again *salvation* may mean being saved from imminent death. Is he then predicting his release? But if he is predicting his release, how could he regard execution as possible?

Moule decides against acquittal on the ground that "the supply of the Spirit" excludes it (22). This reason seems inconclusive. Many commentators, for example Müller, are undecided. Hendriksen dodges the question. He merely notes that "this glorious result will be brought about by *two factors . . . your supplication* and *the help supplied by the Spirit*." One would suppose that the Philippians were praying for his release and if their petitions were granted, as a factor in bringing about some "glorious event," it would be Paul's release. Lenski, referring to Paul's words as a quotation from Job 13:16, holds that neither Job nor Paul had in mind a continuation of his earthly life. Both may or may not be slain. If *salvation* refers to anything on Earth, it is that Paul will be saved from shaming Christ when he speaks before the Roman court.

There is, however, another factor to be considered. Verse 19 is a reason Paul gives for verse 18. "I will rejoice *because* this for me will result toward salvation." What is the *this?* A rapid reading might give and has given some the impression that Paul is referring to his imprisonment and the danger of execution. Another view is that *this* refers to the preaching of Christ by Paul's competitors: "They preach because they are envious, but I rejoice because I see that this advances the Gospel." The word *moi* does not necessarily mean *my* salvation (either temporal or eternal), but "in my case"; that is, these insincere preachers, so far as I am concerned, are advancing the Gospel. In this case the word *salvation* can be that of the converts which the envious preachers have made.

Eadie thinks this is far-fetched; but to me it seems more plausible than the one Eadie proposes. He makes *this* to be a reference to Paul's joyful state of mind. Paul "does not mean . . . the salvation of others . . . or his own. . . . Therefore we understand *touto* to refer to [his] state of mind . . . his joy in the preaching of Christ from whatever motive." This is utter nonsense. It makes the verse say, "I rejoice because this subjective state of mind results in salvation." But it is not his state of mind that produces the encouraging results. It is the preaching itself. *Touto* cannot possibly refer to anything other than the historical circumstances: his imprisonment resulted in an increased preaching of the Gospel.

"The supply of the Holy Spirit" as well as "your prayers" does not determine the interpretation. It fits nearly everything, release from jail, the spread of the Gospel, and even Paul's subjective state of mind.

Now all this–the situation, the prayers, the supply of the Spirit–is according to–not because of, but in conformity with–my expectation and hope. Paul is assured that he who began a good work in him will prevent him from saying anything in his trial that would be shameful, cowardly, or injurious to the name of Christ. This is not bragging, but it is assurance. He expects, hopes, and is sure that he will, as always heretofore, speak boldly. Even now Christ will be magnified whatever happens. Whether Paul lives or dies, his conduct will redound to the glory of Christ. Not many Christians can or should have such assurance. Many of the martyrs may have had. There were Latimer and Ridley who lit a candle that is not yet totally extinguished. Then there was Polycarp whose majestic dedication is often quoted. Polycarp, you remember, also wrote a letter to this same Philippian church. So it was with the martyrs, but it is not so with many of us common folk.

Paul could say such things,

1:21   For to me life is Christ and death is gain.

This verse would need little explanation, were it not that some expositors complicate what seems very simple. They ask, How can it be possible for Christ to be magnified by Paul's death? Eadie reports some involved attempts to describe this *How*. It seems to me that several plausible answers can easily be thought up; but I regard such as peripheral to the verse's basic meaning.

Hendriksen take the *moi* (to me) as a contrast with the previously mentioned envious preachers. This hardly seems possible. Those envious preachers bowed out in verse 18. The present verse is an explanation of verse 20. Paul wants Christ to be magnified either by acquittal or by execution. Why either? Because "so far as I am concerned, life is Christ and death is gain."

Grayston objects that "it is difficult to see why such a piece of personal religion should appear in this particular context" (19). But this particular context, with Paul in jail and in danger of death, is precisely where a personal remark fits best. Martin (76) approves of E. F. Scott's weaker attempt to remove the personal note from the verse. It is thus "narrowly interpreted as an individual and pietistical hope." Paul was no pietist, and pietism is not Christianity; but a professional systematic theologian's emphasis on objective truth does not rule out an apostle's personal remark in these circumstances.

Though the verse is thus easily understood, not every Christian repeats it for himself. Possibly only a few do so. Some years ago, before Gordon Seminary became Gordon-Conwell and moved to South Hampton, Massachusetts, there was a public debate held in the Park Street Church in Boston. Each side had two speakers, but on each side one virtually usurped his colleague's time. The one speaker was the General Secretary of the Ethical Culture Society, and guess who the other was. The subject was ethics. Toward the end the Secretary asked me what conduct I would choose, if I did not accept moral norms as divine. If I were an unbeliever, what would I do? He probably thought that I would break this or that Commandment, but at any rate his question was legitimate. Since we all have to live and act, what actions would we choose if we rejected Christianity?

I prefaced my reply by stating that of course I had no intention of doing what I was about to mention, but if I were an atheist I would shoot myself and save myself a lot of trouble. The Secretary threw up his hands in despair–or defeat.

But the seminary students were equally or even more disturbed. They held a sort of protest rally the next day. At that rally a seminary professor and I offered a defense. The philosophical point was that ethical culture or other non-theistic systems cannot justify the value of life. We do not have to live and act. We can stop living. Can atheism give any reason for condemning suicide? But at any rate the seminary students seemed not to have understood Paul's statement that life is Christ and death is gain. Without Christ there is no value in living. Life is a disappointing, often painful, hardly ever rewarding chore. Why bother? Does the pleasure–if it is pleasure–of watching a baseball game overbalance cancer? Does the memory of a tennis match fifty years ago cure today's arthritis? If in this life only we have hope in Christ, we are of all men most miserable.

1:22 **But if life in the flesh, this is for me a fruit of labor; and what I shall choose, I do not know.**

It is strange how commentators differ. Some say the previous verse is hard to understand, and I think it easy; while Hendriksen says here "The sense is clear enough," and it is not at all clear to me. Since the commentators offer a half dozen different interpretations, one must suspect difficulties somewhere.

Grayston does not really comment on the verse, but he seems to accept the New English Bible's translation: "what if my living on in the body serves some good purpose?" (16). How can this be got from "this to me [is] a fruit of work" is far from clear.

Even if a better translation is proposed, the phrase "a fruit of work" is subject to misinterpretation. The Revised Standard Version and the New International Version say "fruitful labor." This can hardly be correct. When one speaks metaphorically of the fruit of something, the "fruit" almost always designates the result. Hence the fruit of work must be the result of the work. But how can life in the flesh be the result of work in Paul's case? Does it mean that Paul's acquittal will be the result of his own endeavors? Paul will indeed make a defense in court and his acquittal might depend on that defense, but it is hard to suppose that such is the meaning of the verse.

The 1901 American Standard Version translates it, "If to live in the flesh—if this shall bring fruit from my labor, then what I shall choose I know not." Its successor, the New American Standard, has, "If I am to live on in the flesh, this will mean fruitful labor for me; and I do not know which to choose." The reader, even if he knows no Greek, can compare these two with my own crabbed and very literal translation and judge whether the former are satisfactory. One must ask, Can life in the flesh be a fruit of labor? Can a "fruit of labor" be "fruitful labor"?

Martin (73) writes as if he thinks that Paul had a choice between living on and being executed, and did not know which to choose. But Paul had no such choice at all. There was, however, a choice on a distinctly different but closely related matter. Obviously he had a choice between wanting to die and wanting to live. Verse 23 makes this explicitly clear. But this second subject matter is the *desire,* not the fact. The two verses do not seem to have the same reference, and hence the second must not be regarded as a mere repetition of the first.

The simplest explanation of verse 22 seems to be: If I live, I am not sure where I shall go to preach the Gospel.

But there is another complication. The one word *gnōridzō* more often means "I make known" rather than "I know." In this case Paul is telling the Philippians, "I may live, but I do not make my plans known to you." Lenski takes it as "God does not make his plans known to me."

In view of all this, must we not disagree with Hendriksen's blithe confidence that "the sense is clear enough"?

1:23, 24   **But I am hard pressed by the two [alternatives], having the desire for [to set sail] departure and for [to be] being with Christ, for that is better by far; though to remain in the flesh is more necessary for you.**

With respect to grammar Lenski puzzles us. One verse 23 he says, "To indicate the possibility of dying he uses a participle as if this were a minor thing; to express the possibility of living . . . he uses a finite expression. This is not accidental" (745). Whether a participle indicates something of lesser importance is of lesser importance, but of more importance is the fact that there is no finite verb either in the following phrase or in verse 24.

Another linguistic point: The word *depart* of the versions means basically "to set sail." It was then applied to "breaking camp"; and some expositors think Paul used the verb because he was a tent-maker. Hardly plausible: The word already was a euphemism for death.

Although Paul did not control the external situation, he was disturbed as to which of the two outcomes he should prefer. If anything is unclear in this context, it is not Paul's evaluation of the two possibilities: One alternative was better for him, the other for the Philippians and the extension of the Gospel. With regard to the first Eadie makes a most appropriate comparison. Paul looked forward to bliss in Heaven; Socrates could say only, "which of us will come upon a better state is unclear to everyone but God." Let us not condemn Socrates as a reprehensible pagan. Let us pity him for not having received God's revelation. For the theology of the verses, more important than Paul's personal feelings, one notes that Paul's desire to depart is rather inconsistent with any idea of purgatory, and also with the theory of soul-sleep. These verses are neither the only nor the best for maintaining that "the souls of believers are at their death made perfect in holiness and do immediately pass into glory. . . ." But they help to show the consistency of Scripture.

1:25, 26   **And being persuaded of this I know I shall remain and *paramenō* with you all for your furtherance and joy of faith, in order that your boasting may abound in Christ Jesus by me because of my presence again with you.**

The verb *parameno* (a compound of *meno*, remain) means *to stay, to remain alive, serve, continue in office.*

Those two verses raise the question as to whether Paul was actually released from this imprisonment. There are rumors of a second and fatal imprisonment. Between the two Paul may have visited, not only the Philippians again, but also brought the Gospel to Spain. Spain was of course the "extreme west" as Clement of Rome and Chrysostom say. But there is another, though not so likely possibility. Although Spain might be called "the extreme west" by someone in Greece, a Roman, remembering Julius Caesar, might have used the description to indicate Britain. Now there is no archaeological evidence of Paul's having visited either of these two countries. But the constant wars and invasions of Britain could easily have destroyed such evidence, while the more peaceful history of Spain would be more likely to permit its survival if it had ever been there. Romans 15:24, 28 obviously favor Spain, but not conclusively.

The real difficulty in these verses, however, is their seeming inconsistency with the previous verses. Above, Paul seemed to be unsure whether he would be acquitted or not. Here he seems confident that he will be released. Martin (80), with considerable ingenuity, supposes that between Paul's writing the preceding verses and these news came to him of his acquittal, or almost certain acquittal. But 2:17 gives poor support to this guesswork.

Lenski erases the difficulty by denying what the words seem to say. His view is that Paul "does not know absolutely, in an unqualified way." Yet the words sound very confident. Tenney (41, 45) and Grayston (23) dodged the difficulty completely. Motyer (56) asserts his release, but does not harmonize the two passages. Müller (65, 66) treats the present verse as an anticipation that may have not been realized, though he thinks it "more likely he was released." But Paul's words seem to express more than a doubtful anticipation.

At the mention of Paul's coming presence *(parousia)* Eadie launches into an utterly irrelevant disquisition on Christ's *parousia*

(66-68). He admits, however, that Paul "could scarcely have made a stronger asseveration . . . survival, liberation, and proposed visit to the Philippian church." He then asks, "was the apostle's confidence warranted?" (68). "Suffice it to say that [these] difficulties are great." One such is the declaration in Acts 20:25, "And now I know that you all among whom I have gone preaching . . . shall see my face no more." We have then, not only a difficulty of harmonizing verses 20 and 25, but worse, between verse 25 and Acts 20. It may be possible to avoid the first difficulty by assuming that, although Paul knew he would be released, he still had qualms imagining that he would be beheaded, The difficulty with Acts is harder. Eadie describes verse 25 as an "outburst of emotion rather than the utterance of prophetic insight" (69). He notes that 2.17, 23, 24 are less optimistic than 1:25-26. There is also the inconclusive information in Philemon 10, 13, 22.

Likewise inconclusive, and in fact irrelevant, are Eadie's remarks that God did not reveal to Paul ahead of time the details of his missionary journeys, nor did the Spirit prevent lapses of memory. The examples are that Paul expected and planned to go into Bithynia, but the Spirit disapproved of this idea; and as for memory, Paul could not remember how many persons he had baptized in Corinth. These references, however, are totally irrelevant, for Paul, before the journey, never said I shall both go and not go into Bithynia; nor is there any Biblical inconsistency in Paul's forgetting how many he had baptized.

Furthermore the difficulty arising from Acts 20 fades away as one reads the text. Eadie had said, "The apostle's assertion in the preceding paragraph is firm and decided; but we dare not argue upon it, because it comes into direct collision with an assertion as firm and decided in Acts 20:25" (69). This is not so. The "you all among whom I have preached" is limited to the audience Paul is addressing: "you all." Acts simply says that Paul will never again see the people of Ephesus. It has nothing to do with Philippi.

1:27 **Just conduct yourselves worthily of the Gos-**

pel of Christ . . .

Worthily is an adverb, modifying *conduct yourselves,* but it makes poor English. *Conduct yourselves* has as its root the word for *city* or *politics:* Be a citizen worthy of the Gospel–not indeed a citizen of Rome or Philippi, though both cities would be pleased with the mention of citizenship, but of the kingdom of God. However, let us start over again.

1:27 **Be that as it may, conduct yourselves in a manner worthy of the Gospel of Christ, so that whether coming and seeing you, or being absent I may hear of your affairs that you stand [firm] by one Spirit, in one soul struggling [together] in belief of the Gospel . . .**

The exhortation to worthy conduct has as its purpose, or hoped for result, that Paul may see, or receive news of, their steadfastness in the Gospel. The New International Version, following Eadie, has hit upon a happy punctuation, connecting *being absent* with *may hear of you.* Otherwise *coming and seeing you* would as much result in only *hearing about you* as if he had been absent.

The Greek preposition *en* means *by* more often than many commentators think. Here the idea is that the Holy Spirit endows them with the courage to stand firm. That the *pneumati* is not the human spirit is clear by reason of the immediately following reference to the soul or mind. Eadie makes *one soul* epexegetical of *one spirit,* but this just doesn't seem right in spirit of their juxtaposition. The reason is that the verb *stand firm* goes well with in or by *one spirit,* while *one soul* or mind goes well with striving together. Müller makes the strange and indeed self-contradictory remark that "*pneumati* can only [!] allude to the Holy Spirit . . . but must rather be understood here in a general sense as a unity of spirit and insight" (68, note 4). Nor is the matter, though

Chapter One 39

not a major doctrine of systematic theology, so slight as to warrant Lenski's brushing it aside with the remark, "We deem the discussions about the constitutional difference between *pneuma* and *psūche* out of place . . . since both are ethical and not constitutional to man's immaterial part" (753).

Twice in this verse Paul refers to the Gospel: "the Gospel of Christ" and "the belief of the Gospel." The first instance may mean "the Gospel whose source is Christ," or "the Gospel whose subject and content is Christ." But this is pretty much a distinction without a difference. The second instance may mean the faith or belief which is precisely the Gospel–the good news which Christians believe. Eadie definitely opposes this interpretation: "nor can *pistis* signify objectively the system of truth contained in the Gospel–a sense which it never undisputedly has in the New Testament." Well, of course, there is always somebody to dispute anything in the New Testament; but it seems clear to me that *pistis* and *pisteuō* frequently indicate the good news itself.* I think it must mean so here. Paul urges them to strive together, to contend for, not their subjective steadfastness, but their message, the propositions they believe. Consider Paul himself: He does not go around telling the Ephesians and the Corinthians that the Philippians have a firm faith, but that Christ died and rose again. The important

---

* It is irresponsible to assert, "nor can *pistis* signify objectively the system of truth contained in the Gospel–a sense which it never undisputedly has in the New Testament." Granted that *pistis* sometimes designates the subjective activity of believing. Granted also that some texts do not undisputedly refer to the truth of the Gospel. Often, however, the dispute favors the objective sense. But there are other instances where to dispute the objective sense is rather clearly irrational. Presumably but not conclusively objective are (among others) James 2:1; 1 Peter 1:5, 7, 9, and 5:9; Jude 20; Revelation 2:13 and 14:12. But can any unbiased reader believe that all the following refer to the subjective act of believing? Is there not at least one that is undisputedly objective: 1 Timothy 1:2, 4, 19; 2:7, 9, 13; 4:1, 6; 5:8, 12; 6:10, 12, 21; 2 Timothy 3:8; 4:7; Titus 1:4, 13; 2:2; 3:15; 2 Peter 1:1; 1 John 5:4; Jude 3. Please do not ask me to check out a dozen or so more. To say that *pistis* never means the true propositions of the Gospel indicates a disparagement of truth and of the truth.

thing is the objective truth. Lenski is very good here: "Subjective faith is nothing without the objective faith . . . being believers themselves the Philippians defend what they believe . . . to this day the battle is always about the *what"*–something Kierkegaard could not understand.

The fact that Paul mentions the Gospel twice in this verse, and seven other times in the epistle, warrants some explanation of the term. In contemporary preaching it is often misused. I have heard some very conservative Baptists distinguish between the *Gospel* and *church doctrine.* The disciples of Kierkegaard and Barth speak of a *kerygma,* a preaching or announcement, of undetermined content, but of minimum length. Hendriksen expatiates on its meaning for a good five pages. I doubt that a good definition of the Gospel requires five pages, but insistence on the Gospel so defined can stand fifty pages oft repeated. One might say that the Gospel is what Paul preached. Now, what did Paul preach? He himself says, "I am pure from the blood of all men, for I have not shunned to declare unto you all the counsel of God." This includes the five points of Calvinism, the TULIP, and is not restricted to the five points of fundamentalism: inerrancy, incarnation, miracles, substitutionary death, and bodily resurrection. These latter are an essential and indispensable part of the Gospel, but they are not the whole of it. The Gospel includes the P of the TULIP, the perseverance of the saints as Philippians just said back in verse six. In fact the Gospel is the entire Bible, from which nothing should be subtracted nor to which nothing should be added. Although no minister, not even Paul, can preach the whole Gospel in one sermon, a prolonged reluctance to declare it all prevents a minister from being free from the blood of his auditors.

The several versions usually translate *one soul* as *one mind.* The use of *one man* in the New International Version, and especially in the New English Bible is not defensible, though even so they make clear what the principle of ecumenicity should be. Paul here and elsewhere insists on theological unity, not a mere organizational union of different doctrinal positions. Recall that in 1

Corinthians 1:10 his exhortation is, "you all say the same thing." Nor does the word *say* imply that they are to *think* differently, for he adds, "in the same mind and in the same judgment." Such verses as these show how deplorably the fortunes of Christianity have declined since the sixteenth and seventeenth centuries. One publisher refused a manuscript of mine because it did not take a "mediating" (ambiguous, equivocal) position. That publisher would certainly have held Augustus Toplady in contempt. Dear reader, get his complete works and study them. I do not agree with his Lockean philosophy, but his theology, like *Rock of Ages,* now defaced in Pentecostal hymn books, is of the best.

1:28 **... and not being frightened in any way by the opponents, which is an indication to them of destruction, but of your salvation, and this from God ...**

Of course the New American Standard gives a smoother translation: "in no way alarmed by your opponents–which is a sign to them of destruction, but of salvation for you, and that too from God."

Some commentators spend time deciding whether the opponents were Jews or Gentiles. The former are the more mistaken, for there were few if any Jews in Philippi. But the latter are also mistaken if they mean that the Gentiles were the only opponents. Paul's wording is completely general. It is probable, however, that Paul had the Gentiles chiefly in mind, for in verse 30 he refers to a conflict which he had in Philippi, which the Philippians had witnessed, and which is described in Acts 16:12-40. This event is an appropriate example of not being scared.

The courage of the Philippians will be an indication, an evidence, a pointer, but hardly a proof, to them of [their] destruction. The word *autois* (to them) is hardly doubtful; but the correct reading in the next phrase presents a puzzle. The question involved is: To whom is what a sign? Some manuscripts read *umōn* (*your* salvation). With this reading the courage of the Philippians is a sign to the opponents of "your salvation" as well as of "their destruction." It is not a sign to the Philippians of their salvation. The sign in both cases is a sign to the adversaries. But there is another reading: Tischendorf indicates that A, B, C read *umōn* (your), while D, E, F, K, L read *umin* (to you). This reading gives a smoother sense: The Philippian courage is a sign of destruction to the opponents, but a sign of salvation to the Philippians. The King James version has "to you"; the more recent versions have "your salvation"–a sign to the opposition. Eadie prints *umōn,* of you; but then he inserts a "to you." The Textus Receptus and King James are more easily understood, for the pagans would hardly understand the Christians' firmness to be a sign that the Christians were saved. The translators, however, favor the harder reading on the ground that the scribes are more likely to make the original easier to understand than harder.

In any case, the salvation, the destruction, the firmness, and the sign are all from God. To limit the word *this (touto)* to any one of these violates the thought. Grammatically the demonstrative *touto* can refer to the word *sign,* for neuter demonstratives often refer to feminine nouns. But the intelligible meaning whch the sign signifies is the entire context. Paul wants to say, "the whole thing is from God." A treatise on the sovereignty of God could well use this verse.

1:29, 30   **... for to you was the grace given, on behalf of Christ not only to believe in him but also to suffer for him, with the same agony such as you saw in me and now heard in [about] me.**

The sentence began at verse 27, and its complications increase into the crescendo of these final two verses. Even a deliberately literal translation has to polish it up somewhat.

The first word, *oti,* most frequently means *because* and states the reason for the preceding assertion. For example, "*Because* the foolishness of God is wiser than men, Christ is the wisdom of God" (1 Corinthians 1:25, 24), Or, "We preach Christ Jesus . . . *because* God has shined in our hearts" (2 Corinthians 4:5, 6). On the other hand, *oti* can be consecutive, introducing some pertinent fact, but not strictly a cause. For example, "what sort of a man is this, that the winds and the sea obey him?" (Matthew 8:27). Or, "what sign do you show us, seeing that you do these things?" (John 2:18). One cannot translate this as, "Because you have done these things, you therefore have shown or will show us a sign." The antecedent is a question, not a statement of fact that needs an explanation. Indeed, Jesus refused them the sort of sign they asked for.

Now, does this verse in Philippians mean, "*Because* God favored you with persecution, therefore this is of God"? Does it mean, "*Because* God favored you, therefore such is a sign to your adversaries"? And surely not "this is of God *because* God favored you." Such would be plain tautology.

Seeing that the causal usage does not quite fit, we had better translated it "seeing that." But the two uses overlap somewhat because we had better translated it one way because the causal usage does not quite fit.

The antecedent is not just the phrase, "This is from God," for the *this* itself takes us further back, possibly all the way back in this complicated sentence to its beginning in verse 27, but at least to verse 28.

In addition to the *oti* and its antecedent, the grammar of verses 29 and 30 is tortuous. Apparently Paul intended to write: "God gave you the grace to suffer for Christ"; then his rapid-fire mind added the idea that their belief in Christ was also a gift from God. And so the sentence increased from six lines to ten.

Faith is a gift of God, for as Ephesians 2:8 says, "By grace you have been saved through faith, and that [faith, or that salvation by faith] not of yourselves, it is the gift of God." That faith or any other comfortable circumstance is a gracious gift of the divine providence is plausible. But people are less likely to see agony as a gracious gift. It is rather a "gift" we would rather not be given. Yet remember that Peter and the apostles "departed from the council, rejoicing that they were counted worthy to suffer shame for his name" (Acts 5:41). Paul also said the same thing about himself: "I rejoice in my sufferings for your sake, and in my flesh I do my share on behalf of his body . . . in filling up that which is lacking in Christ's afflictions" (Colossians 1:24. Compare my commentary on the same verse to avoid a misunderstanding.)

Paul encourages the Philippians in their suffering by calling to their attention the fact that they and he suffer the *same* agony. Well, it was indeed *agony,* even though the Greek word *agōn* means only a struggle.

CHAPTER TWO

2:1, 2   If then there be any help in Christ, if any consolation of love, if any common possession of the Spirit, if any affections and compassions, fill my joy by thinking the same thing, having the same love, together in soul thinking the one thing . . .

One or two grammatical points make these verses difficult to translate, though the meaning is relatively clear. We must remember that koinē Greek, compared with the classical language, was just plain sloppy. The distinctions that had made meaning unmistakable were now lost. Ambiguity flourished. Contemporary American, in which many people cannot distinguish between the nominative *I* and the accusative *me,* is an even worse example of a descent into barbarism. Furthermore, Paul himself had little literary flair, and with his extremely keen and active mind his sentences are distressingly complex.

The first of two difficulties comes in the phrase "if any affections and compassions." The *any* is masculine singular, while *affections* is neuter plural and *compassions* is masculine plural. Why then the singular *tis*? That *tis* is correct and that the plural *tina* is not the correct reading can hardly be disputed. But those who insist on *tis* usually fail to provide an explanation. At most they remark that it is natural, when one begins with a singular three times running, to use it the fourth time. I suggest in addition that *affections and compassions* is–note the singular–a simple phrase, and taken as a whole permits the singular *any.*

There is a second strictly grammatical difficulty, but first let us

45

straighten out the connection between verse one and verse two. Lenski emphatically defends the singular *tis* against any textual critics who would change it to the plural *tina*. But further, condemning the usual versions, he denies that verse 2 is the apodosis of the conditions in verse 1, and he makes them two separate sentences. Verse 1, he says, has its own apodosis: "If accordingly [there] is any admonition, [let it be] in connection with Christ" etc. (761). His reason is that otherwise "the thought is disjointed. . . . The protases do not match the apodosis." There is some truth to this. At least the apodoses do not come by strictly syllogistic form. But then the versions do not strictly make them such. For one thing, the so-called apodoses are commands and not propositions. But this does not make them disjointed as Lenski holds. Furthermore, if these commands are rephrased into propositions, such as, "you ought to increase my joy" in the way described, and if one inserts a few extra premises that Paul has taken for granted, one will find that the whole is a valid sorites. We all, Lenski included, take premises for granted and argue in enthymemes. This involves a certain danger of course, but then complete syllogisms are not always valid either.

The second grammatical difficulty comes in verse 2. It is the conjunction *ina*. In classical Greek *ina* was emphatically purposive: *in order that*. One would have to search many pages of Xenophon, Demosthenes, Plato, and Aristotle, or of Homer, Hesiod, and Euripides to find *ina* introducing a result clause. In Hellenistic Greek, however, *ina* often blatantly introduces a result clause. Since this grammatical point affects the meaning of the verse, the discussion can wait until we get there.

In verse 1, then, the New English Bible translated the first phrase, "If then our common life in Christ yields anything to stir the heart." Aside from other matters, this loose paraphrase renders the one word *paraclēsis* as "anything that stirs the heart." There is no justification for this whatever. The other modern versions usually choose *encouragement,* while the commentators often have *admonition* or *exhortation*. Of these, *encouragement* is surely the best. Remembering that the Paraclete is the *helper* or *advocate,* one could as well use the word *help:* "if there is any *help* in Christ." One might stretch the Greek and say, "If there is any help *from* Christ." The sense is, "if Christ be the source of any help." Eadie rejects *by, on account of,* and the idea of *source.* His reasoning is so obscure that I have difficulty in identifying, for quotation, which of his sentences are supposed to be his reason. Hence, "if Christ be the source of any help," or "if any help is to be found in Christ" makes good sense and is a tolerable translation. It seems to me that the word *help* is better than *encouragement* as the modern versions have it, because mere encouragement, a cheering section as it were, is sometimes not much of a help

Although the phrase "consolation of love" does not include the words "in Christ," it makes good sense so to understand it. *Christ* is in the previous phrase and there is no good reason to exclude it here. Müller thinks otherwise and writes, "If there is any stimulus or incentive of love: 'if love has any persuasive power to move you to concord.' " To this he adds a footnote: "Rightly, incentive (RSV), encouragement, not *consolation* (ASV)" (73). Arndt and Gingrich says, "encouragement, especially as consolation, alleviation, . . . if there is any solace afforded by love, Phil. 2:1." Hence Müller's attempt to rule out *consolation* is defective. Furthermore, although it is not too clear, Müller and others speak as if the love were some human emotion. Hendriksen very clearly refers to whatever love existed among the Philippians themselves. To me this seems totally incongruous with the context. Christ is in the previous phrase, the Spirit in the following phrase. Can we now exclude them and replace them here with the Philippians? Even if one say that the Spirit indwelt the Philippians, it is still the Spirit.

"Any community of S– or s–pirit": What does it mean? Does it mean merely that the Philippians think alike? Or does it mean that the Holy Ghost is common to them? The word *koinōnia* was discussed in 1:15. It means that two or more persons have something in common. Here what they have is the Holy Spirit. It cannot mean intellectual agreement or identity of belief. Of course, several expositors think so. But consider a similarity Motyer discovered (67). His, in my opinion, is not one of the best commentaries, but here he hit the jackpot. "Note that the order of the first three items in the verse is the same as that in the 'grace' in 2 Corinthians 13:14, viz., Christ ... love ... Spirit. Indeed, the concluding phrase, 'fellowship of the Spirit' is virtually identical. May it not be, therefore, that Paul is reminding the Philippians here of the great Trinitarian activity of salvation whereby we are 'in Christ,' experience the reality of God's love, and have been woven into a fellowship of which the Holy Spirit is both Author and indweller?" Lenski reduces the whole matter to the human relationships among the Philippians themselves; but these do not seem to me to provide sufficient force to the imperatives of verse 2. He explicitly denies that the Holy Spirit is in view, and demotes the meaning to spiritual fellowship among the Philippians. He speaks of "admonitions from each other" (764), "consolation from each other," and "clinging close together." The whole is strictly on a human level.

Verse 2 obviously descends to the human level and urges the Philippians to do certain things because of the preceding considerations. Apparently Paul could count on the devotion of the Philippians toward him, and hence could ask them to fill him with joy. We may not suppose, however, that this was his real motive. He chiefly had in mind the advancement of the Philippians in their degree of sanctification. How then may one so advance? Or in this case, how can a group of Christians so advance?

The first thing is not overt conduct. While a pastor must lay a certain emphasis on behavior, he must insist that action results from thought. At least correct action results from correct thinking, and action without thought can be disastrous. Hence Paul urges his converts to think the same thing. Of course this same thing is not a belief in the Olympian deities. The thing they are to be agreed upon is the Gospel of Christ as Paul had preached it.

Without this theological basis, their conduct would range from bad to worse. In these immediate verses Paul does not specify the several doctrines: He gave one back in 1:6 and another very important belief will come up in 2:6-11.

His second command is to have the same love. *Agapē* was mentioned in 1:9, 17. It is a love that abounds in knowledge. As was said above on the first of these two verses, love consists in obedience to the law of God. Hence the law must be known and understood. This intellectual note continues to sound: "together in soul thinking the one thing."

The words *to en* are peculiar, particularly the article. If Paul had said, "thinking one thing," we would have easily understood him to mean unity of doctrine. But *the* one thing seems to single out something in particular. Lenski translates it, "minding this one thing," which he identifies as the following verses. Lenski's view is at least plausible because, contrary to the King James, Revised Standard Version, New International Version, and New American Standard, there can be no period at the end of verse 2. Eadie wants to understand *to en* as *to auto,* which would be more easily understood, but while some manuscripts have *to auto, to en* has the superior attestation. Hendriksen, translating it as "setting your minds on unity," takes *to en* as abstract or general, and not as requiring a specific example. Nonetheless the grammar, though difficult, seems to require verses 3, 4 as the reference.

We seem to have passed over the second grammatical difficulty, left dangling a bit ago. "The same love," "the one thing," are parts of the *ina* clause. Now, rather obviously the verse cannot mean, "fill my joy in order that you may think alike." This would be backwards. If there must be some notion of purpose, it would have to say, "Think, or believe, the same doctrines in order that my joy may be complete." The text actually says, "Complete my joy that you agree" in doctrine. The only classical remnant here is that *phronetē* (think) is subjunctive. Even as an objective clause after a verb of wishing or desiring, "I desire you to make me happy by your doctrinal unity," it is an awkward construction.

Blass and Debrunner say that in consecutive clauses "*ina* can be substituted for the infinitive of result (probably also for other kinds too, in later writers) but hardly for actual result, e.g. 1 John 1:9, 'He is faithful and just *ina* he forgave (aorist subjunctive) us" (Blass and Debrunner, § 391, 5). They give us the interesting German example: Er schlief ein, um nicht wieder aufzumachen: He fell asleep (in order) never to waken again.

2:3, 4 **... nothing through strife or vanity, but in humility considering each other better than yourselves, not seeking each one their own [advantage], but also everyone the [good] of others.**

These two verses are so clear that comments are hardly necessary. One ought not, however, picture the Philippian church as extraordinarily remiss in conduct. Nor should we think that the women mentioned in 4:2 motivated Paul in these verses. It is better to take the passage as general teaching. In this way we of the twentieth century may find more profit. It will be noted that the dishonorable conduct condemned here is not so much overt action as it is inward motivation. While all too many church-goers are lax in their actions, some very conscientious souls are extremely concerned. They want to live a Christian life, and very diligently examine proposed courses of action. Does the law of God forbid so and so? Is this or that permitted? Should we avoid every "appearance" (a mistaken translation) of evil?

Those who are so troubled should study ethics systematically. For example, ordinary pagan ethics in ancient Greece, as Aristotle reveals, put stress on pride. To be properly respected and admired by the public, one had to "keep up with the Joneses." If your neighbor invites you to a social occasion, you must in due time throw a more splendid party.

From Paul's Christian point of view the evil here is not so much the actual party: Indeed the party could fulfil, outwardly, all the

New Testament's requirements for decorum. The evil lies in the motivation. To bring it closer to home, one can sin by doing some very good and commendable church work. For, although certain types of acts are sinful no matter what the conditions may be, murder for example, other types are good or bad simply because of the motive. Even the ploughing of the wicked is sin.

Christian ethics therefore has a double criterion: the external act and the internal motive. An evil act done with a good motive is bad; a good act done with a wrong motive is also bad. As a college professor teaching Christian students, I have found a number of conscientious sudents painfully perplexed about practical problems. Recognition of the double criterion will solve some of their difficulties.

Paul here is insisting on right motives. Strife and vanity spoil the best of actions. Humility is necessary. We must think of ourselves as less sanctified than the other members of the congregation. Even if the public knows that so and so has committed such and such a sin, we must still beware that we have committed a worse though less obvious sin. Or, if sin is not at all the question, and the matter has to do with organizing some congregational activity, one must consider the possibility that another's plan for the picnic might possibly be better than one's own.

If, however with due humility we are convinced that our plan is better, and especially if we are solidly convinced that his plan is sinful, we must of course oppose it. Paul himself, you will remember, did not accept Barnabas' plan, nor did he seem so humble when he sternly rebuked the Galatian Judaizers. He and John pointedly condemned the false prophets. In some places and in some eras condemnation has been overdone; but in this twentieth century the churches have erred in the opposite direction.

That balance is required, is clear from the word *also* in verse 4: It does not say "not seeking, each one, their own [advantage]" period. It adds, "but *also* everyone the good of others." Human nature, depraved as it is, automatically neglects the good of others and seeks personal aggrandizement. Now, Paul does not tell

52 Philippians

us to forget our own good. In fact it would be sin to do so. But we must not seek our own good only; we must *also,* everyone of us, seek the good of others. If we have a good grasp of the Christian theory of ethics, we shalll realize at least philosophically if not practically that our good and our neighbor's good coincide.

2:5   Let this be thought by you which also [was thought] by Christ Jesus . . .

There is a textual problem here which the reader may skip over if he wishes. The verb *think* in the Textus Receptus is in the passive voice, as in the translation above. A few uncials and almost all cursives have this passive verb. The main uncials have an active verb. Yet neither the footnotes in the Aland critical text nor Metzger's *Textual Commentary* mentions this fact. The two words *en umin* (in you, or, by you) are hard to translate if the verb is active, for it is active imperative. "Think in yourselves" would make sense, but unfortunately *umin* does not mean *yourselves.* The New International Version's *attitude* is too loose a paraphrase; and the Revised Standard Version's "among yourselves" faces two difficulties: (1) Eadie correctly notes that "The phrase *en umin* is not 'among you' nor is it in any sense superfluous. It points out the inner region of thought which this feeling is to occupy" (95); and (2) "yourselves," as just indicated, is a mistranslation. Of course no one expects accuracy in the New English Bible, which has, "let your bearing towards one another arise out of your life in Christ Jesus."

Martin (95) writes, "Grayston gives the admirable rendering: 'Think this way among yourselves, which also you think in Christ Jesus, i.e. as members of his church.' . . ."* For several reasons this is a virtually impossible interpretation. First there is the awkward "among yourselves." Second, and far more important, Martin's idea is that the Philippians are to think among them-

---

* I cannot find this sentence in Grayston.

selves as they also think as members of Christ's church. Not only is this tautologous, but worse, it cannot fit into what follows. The context requires the idea that the Philippians are to think in humility as Christ also thought in humility. The next verse will describe how Christ thought and acted, not how the Philippians should think and act. The words of 2:6-8 would be utter nonsense and indubitably false if attributed to the Philippians. They give Christ's thought. As Motyer so clearly says, "But rarely does Scripture open to us the thought and motives of the Son of God as he contempleated the cross, and this is the speciality of these verses."

A commentary may also add a remark directed to some actual deficiencies in the churches of the late twentieth century. Many ministers and congregations, not otherwise infected with extreme liberalism, have become more anthropocentric than theocentric. Their emphasis is on emotion and feeling, rather than on the truth of God. The defense they give is that they are "practical," not theoretical. Christianity means a life rather than a doctrine. To be sure, this chapter and other Philippian verses are exhortations to moral conduct. But where else, better than here, is the doctrinal basis for conduct expressed? Thought controls conduct, and wrong throughts produce wrong conduct. That indeed is why Paul here says, Think as Christ thought. There can be no morality without theology.

What is worse, the so-called para-church organizations, groups that refuse to obey Paul's commands in the Pastoral Epistles, seem to be little interested even in morality. I do not refer to the recently discovered sexual immorality among the staff of one such group, but rather to their open mode of operation. In one typical case, after "converting" a girl in twenty minutes by their psychological expertise, they came back to her a few weeks later and asked, "Do you still have the joy?" Emotions count; repentance is denied; morality or righteousness is ignored; and truth is scorned.

2:6, 7 ... **who, being in the form of God, did not consider it robbery to be equal with God, but**

**emptied himself, taking the form of a slave,
coming to be in the likeness of men . . .***

Here begins one of the greatest passages in the New Testament, a passage describing the nature of Jesus Christ. It is also one of the hardest, perhaps *the* hardest outside the book of Revelation, to understand. One commentator warns, "In this important, and it is to be feared much perverted passage, nearly every word has formed the subject of controversy." It will test one's stamina, devotion, and obedience to the command to meditate on God's word day and night. A few points are not so difficult; the whole is exceedingly important; and Lenski says, "Note it well."

Even the first word *who* has occasioned dispute, though the question raised is, I believe, easily answered. The relative *who,* of course, refers to *Christ Jesus,* which it immediately follows. The question, however, was whether it referred to the Son in his pre-incarnate state or to Jesus as he walked on Earth. The Greek

---

* Possibly it was Kohmeyer who first concluded, a bit after World War I, that verses 6-11 were poetry, a hymn composed by some unknown Christian writer in the first century, whom Paul quoted. Many critics have adopted this view. Grayston, *The Letter of Paul to the Philippians* (Cambridge at the University Press, 1967, 21-23) states, "Verses 6-11, especially in Greek, have the arrangement and style of poetry . . . an original hymn," and he discusses its possible sources.

Of course if the verses were a hymn they would have to have the style and arrangement of poetry "especially in Greek." But the Greek of these verses does not have the arrangement of poetry. They cannot be scanned! Nor do the verses have the right number of syllables per line to match up with Grayston's stanzas. The numbers in Grayston's first stanza are, 9, 15, 8, 6, 13, 11, 8, 12; his second stanza in Greek goes, 8, 19, 10, 5, 16, 12, 10, 7. And when Grayston agrees that the phrase "death on the cross" is an insertion and "breaks the rhythm," the reply is, there was no rhythm to break. We can sing, in modern Greek
 Sun Christō, Sun Christō, phobos ou thanou,
 Sun Christō asphaleia, chara pantou.
But no one can sing Philippians 2:6-11.

fathers, stressing the next noun, *morphē*, insisted that Paul had the eternal, pre-incarnate Son in mind. Later exegetes stress his earthly ministry, perhaps stress it too much, or at least obscure too much his eternal being. It seems to me that the passage begins with his original deity and then speaks of his earthly life. Neither can be wholly omitted, but though his earthly life is integral to the argument, the later exegetes may have too much obscured his equality with God.

The ancient view seeks support in the word *morphē* (form). Chrysostom says, "the form of God is the *nature* of God." Gregory of Nyssa, in the same vein, said, "The *form* of God is absolutely the same as the *essence*" or being of God. Now, these men and other early fathers were Greeks, Greek was their native language, and if they said that *morphē* means *nature* or *essence,* who are we, poorly educated Americans, or better educated Britishers, who are we to contradict them?*

Nevertheless there are difficulties. First, there are terminological difficulties. Discussions on the Trinity have, over the centuries, utilized the words *nature, essence, being, substance, subsistence,* and the very unfortunate Latin term *person.* These are hardly ever defined with precision. For example, one would ordinarily

---

* If we stress *nature* or *essence,* we can avoid a mistake that Augustine made and a mistake that W. G. T. Shedd made in correcting Augustine. In a footnote to *De Trinitate,* I, vi, 12, Shedd says, "In Phil. 2:6 *God* must surely denote the Divine Essence, not the First Person of the Essence. St. Paul describes 'Christ Jesus' as subsisting *(uparchōn)* ... in a form of God, not *the* form. St. Paul refers to one of the three forms. ... Had the apostle employed the article with *morphē,* the implication would be that there is only one 'form of God,' that is, one Person in the Divine Essence. If this *theou* denotes the Father, as Augustine says, St. Paul would teach that the Logos subsisted 'in a form of the Father,' which would imply that the Father had more than one form."

To which we answer, Augustine is surely wrong in making Christ a form of the Father. In this Shedd's criticism is well taken. But his remarks on the article and the assertion that God has three forms, and that Paul refers to one of these forms, are more than doubtful.

think that a *person* must have a *will*. But the orthodox doctrine allows the three Persons of the Trinity to have only one will among them, while surprisingly the incarnate Jesus has two wills and yet is not a human *person*. Nestorianism, with its assertion that Christ was two persons, is considered a heresy. Other theologians, orthodox or otherwise, distinguish between the *substance* of God and his *nature*. But would not a substance without a nature lack all attributes? And would not a substance without attributes or characteristics be a blank nothing? Enough: We are straying too far from the exegesis of Philippians.

Yet one of the difficulties in Philippians is that we must use some of these words. The question was, Can we agree with Chrysostom and Gregory in identifying *form* and *essence?* There is a plausible, let us not say a conclusive, reason for thinking that they were mistaken. God's *essence, being, definition,* or *nature* never changes. God is eternal and immutable. Yet the following verse *seems* to say that Christ discarded one *morphē* and took another one, the *morphē* of a slave. Now, if *morphē* means merely an *appearance,* the difficulty is greatly diminished, but if *morphē* means *essence* or *nature,* the Christ stopped being God. Is this possible? Can God undeify himself? Is he not immutable? Where would be the Trinity, if one of them disappeared? For this reason, and because it seems unlikely that Paul would have given different meanings to the same word in two consecutive verses, various exegetes reject the meaning of *definition* or *essence* in its first instance. But then, if this is so, what meaning fits both instances?

The word *morphē* itself often denotes the visible shape of an object. This is impossible here, even if it must have the same meaning in both instances, because the present verse refers to Christ's pre-incarnate state. This must be so because Paul here applies the term to Christ as he was before he humbled or emptied himself. The *kenosis,* as it is called (though the noun does not occur in the New Testament and seems rare even in classical Greek), comes only in the following verse, and hence *morphē* cannot refer to physical form or appearance, even if this should require the two instances to have different meanings. If verse 6 does not define the meaning of the term as such, it certainly specifies what the *morphē* is: The specific *morphē* is equality with God, "who being in the form of God did not consider it robbery to be equal to God." But then if Christ was eternally equal to God, could he undeify himself? Can God become non-god?

But wait; we are going too fast. Does the verse really say that Christ was equal with God? Müller objects to translating the phrase as "to be equal to God." He argues that equality with God would require a masculine singular *isos,* but the text has a neuter plural *isa.* "Where this difference is not noted, the two expressions *en morphē theou uparchōn* and *to einai isa theō* are wrongly considered identical in meaning. For this reason the Vulgate rendering *esse se aequalem Deo* cannot be deemed correct" (79, note 4).

On the other hand, Rienecker's *Linguistic Key* (not a commentary) says, "*isos* equal, exactly equal. ... The neuter plural can be used here as an adverb which in turn is used here as an adjective. ... The accusative is used with the articular infinitive, 'to be equal with God' " (204).

In defense of the usual interpretation one may say that if *isa* were used adverbally (to be equally God), the noun *God* would have to be nominative, not dative as it actually is.

If, now, we agree that Christ is the equal of God and that therefore *morphē* means *essence* or *definition,* the difficulty that arises depends on the idea that the *kenosis* consists in discarding one form and assuming a different form. A careful reading of the text shows that this assumption has no basis. The text does not say that Christ discarded his pre-incarnate form. It says that he humbled himself by adding to himself a second form. Adding this second form was indeed a humiliation, but it was not suicide. The person, nature, or essence remained.

Several authors try to straddle the problem, not willing completely to deny deity to Jesus, but having him in some way set aside his divine prerogatives. Rienecker speaks peculiarly when he says, "Perhaps the meaning is that Christ did not use his equality with God in order to snatch or gain power and dominion, riches and pleasure, worldly glory" (204). Now it is plainly evident that Jesus did not use whatever power he had to snatch riches or earthly glory from the Jews or the Romans. But the verb *snatch,* if we use it to translate *arpagmon* (robbery), does not refer to Jesus in Palestine, but to the Son in Heaven. Not earthly glory, but equality with God was what the Son did not have to snatch. He did not think it necessary to grasp at it because he already was eternally God's equal. Hence Rienecker's suggestion, if that is what he really meant, that the Son did not think earthly glory something to be snatched at, is most peculiar.

Another theologian asserts that Jesus "emptied himself by giving up the independent exercise of his relative attributes. Thus he was omniscient, omnipotent, and omnipresent as the Father granted him the exercise of these attributes" (Henry C. Thiessen, *An Outline of Lectures in Systematic Theology,* mimeographed second edition, 144; chapter on "Soteriology, The Nature of the Incarnation").

Two points may be noted here. First–but the lesser in importance for the exegesis of the epistle though of greater importance for theology as a whole–it is not clear why omniscience is a "relative" attribute. In one sense all attributes are relative–relative to each other. None stands outside of all relation. Similarly, though Thiessen does not precisely say so for himself, he seems to identify holiness, love, and truth as "immanent" attributes. But as omniscience can be viewed as immanent, why cannot love be viewed as relative? Then, second, Christ never exercised any trinitarian attributes independently of the Father. To suppose so would be to deny the unity of the Godhead. Hence, if there had never been any independent exercise, it could not have been given up.

As for the more radical assertion that Christ ceased to exercise even one of his attributes, the New Testament records instances of his exercising various divine attributes during his earthly ministry without indicating that he ceased to exercise even one. If anyone should say that the so-called nature miracles (stilling the storm) do not require the direct power of God, since perhaps God could have sent an angel to do something similar, yet Hebrews 1:3 rather clearly ascribes the upholding of all things, that is, the preservation of the universe as a whole, to the incarnate Christ. Consider also John 1:9 where it says that Christ enlightens every man who comes into the world. Men were being born during Jesus' earthly life; therefore he engaged in that divine epistemological activity while in the form of man. John also attributes omniscience to him in 2:24, 25. Then there is Colossians 2:9. During his earthly ministry there dwelt in him all the fulness of the Godhead bodily. The reader, instead of solving crossword puzzles, might entertain himself by searching out other verses on the subject.

Müller gives a clear and excellent account of the devastation that the *kenosis* theory would wreak on the truth of the Bible. He makes five points which can be abbreviated as follows:

(1) The kenotic theory annuls the doctrine of the Trinity by having one of the Three Persons ceasing to be omniscient and omnipotent for a time.

(2) Obviously this violates the doctrine of immutability. It introduces, not changes in the course of predestinated history, but changes into the subjective state of God's mind.

(3) Discarding divine attributes destroys the deity of Christ. A man who is not omniscient cannot be God, nor can one who is not omnipresent.

(4) It makes impossible Christ's role as a mediator. To mediate he must be both God and man; but a person who is not omniscient is not God.

(5) The kenotic theory contradicts the Creed of Chalcedon, the Augsburg Confession, the Belgic Confession, and the Westminster Confession. These of course are not Scripture, but they are the best summaries of Christian doctrine ever formulated.

As a sort of conclusion for a discussion that could be considerably extended, it is interesting to note how the Right Reverend Charles J. Ellicott tries hard to avoid identifying *morphē* as *essence* or *nature*. But he admits that

> *en morphe theou* [in the form of God] and *to einai isa theō* [to be equal to God] are virtually, though not precisely, identical. Both refer to the Divine nature, the former, however, (perhaps with a momentary glance of thought to its *aulia* [immateriality], points to it in respect of its form and preexistence; the latter with exquisite distinction, to its *state* and *present continuance,* referring to the very moment of the *egēsatō*. On *these* premises the translation would be, 'He thought the being equal to God no act of robbery'–no usurpation of any dignity which was not his own by right of nature (55).

2:7 **... but emptied himself, taking the form of a slave, coming to be in the likeness of men ...**

In the involved exegesis of verse 6, it was necessary to use some of verse 7. Now, without repeating too much of the preceding, the account will continue with what was omitted.

The first point is the verb *emptied.* In the preceding discussion it became clear that the *Logos* did not divest himself of one form in order to assume another form. Motyer is only half right: "We cannot avoid the question which is as logical as it is enticing– emptied himself of what? ... In point of fact, however, to ask of what he emptied himself is to be guided by logic rather than by the course which these verses themselves take" (80). Motyer apparently does not like to think logically. If the verse had said that Christ discarded one thing to assume another, it would be quite logical to ask what. But if the verse does not say that he discarded something, the question is illogical, not logical as Motyer says. The logical exetetical problem is to determine what the verb *emp-*

tied means. Obviously it is metaphorical. Literally Christ emptied himself, or he was emptied of some blood while on the cross, and the next verse mentions it. But this is not the meaning of the present verse, for it says, "he emptied himself," not "he shed his blood." In the realization that the usage is metaphorical, the French translation has "il s'est anéanti," (he annihilated himself); but this is even worse than "he emptied himself." It seems to me best to take the two following participial clauses as definitory of the metaphor: He emptied himself, that is, he took the form of a slave.

The phrase, "the form of a slave," conjures up in the minds of many people the service Jesus rendered to the people he healed and helped. Actually that is not the meaning at all. He whom he served was God the Father. Jesus was not the servant of men, but he came to serve God in the manner described in the next verse.

The Revised Standard Version mistranslates the second participle: It does not mean *to be born*. The very same participle occurs again in the next verse, in the phrase "coming to be subject to death." While Christ's humiliation included his incarnation, the latter is no more indicated here than his other human limitations. *Humiliation* is a good word, and if the King James is not a literal tranlation, it is the best interpretation of the metaphorical meaning.

The Lutherans use this verse to support their doctrine of the *communicatio idiomatum* (the possession in common of attributes). They believe that the Person of Crhist so unifies his two natures that the human attributes become attached to the divine nature–an idea that seems utterly absurd to me–and that also the divine attributes attach themselves to Christ's human nature. This is essential to their doctrine of consubstantiation. Luther put it more bluntly than perhaps modern Lutherans would like: In the eucharist, he said, we chew the body of Christ with our teeth. That this be possible, it is necessary to attribute omnipresence or ubiquity to Christ's physical body, so that his body may be in many places all around the world at the same time. But if Christ's body were ubiquitous by nature, it would be everywhere always, and we would be eating it at every meal. Not only so, but pagans would be eating it too.

A Calvinist can only regret that the Lutheran churches retained the one doctrine on which Luther disagreed with Zwingli and Calvin, and discarded, under the influence of Melanchthon, the many doctrines on which there was complete or almost complete agreement at the beginning.

A quotation from Lenski will substantiate these remarks so far as the exegesis of Philippians is concerned.

The matter is perfectly plain: in the incarnation the human nature which Christ Jesus assumed was made partaker of all that belonged to the divine nature of Christ. The dogmaticians term this the *genus majestaticum* of the *communicatio idiomatum* as taught throughout Scripture. By this communication and by a participation in virtue of the *unio personalis* of the two natures the human nature existed and exists "in God's form." Only those who cancel this personal union of Christ's natures can say that only the logos in Christ has existence "in God's form" and not the human nature he assumed. The logos has this existence "in God's form" as God, and because he is very God was this gift from all eternity; his human nature has it by gift and communication since its assumption. Thus Paul writes of "Christ Jesus": "existing in God's form" (776).

A note is needed on the four words, "coming to be in the likeness of men"–four words in Greek. The word *likeness* is less definite than *equal* or *form*. The Son was the equal of God, but he was not identical to men. For one thing, he was sinless. For another, as said before, he was not a human person, however much he was like a human person. He got tired and hungry; and the next verse will mention another similarity. But for the moment we must see that *omoiomatī* is something less than identity. Romans 8:3 says that God sent his Son in the *omoiomatī* of sinful flesh. This does not mean that Jesus sinned. He appeared to sin; at least the Pharisees charged him with many sins. So he came in the *likeness,* but not in the reality, of sinful flesh.

2:7, 8 ... **and having been found schematized as a man he humbled himself, becoming obedient even to death, indeed death on a cross** ...

I do not know why the critical edition puts the first phrase into verse seven; the versions, even the New English Bible and Revised Standard Version, make these words the beginning of verse 8. The latter makes much better sense because the phrase does not fit what precedes: It fits into what follows it.

Meyer and a few others (the editors of the critical text?) connect the phrase with what precedes, placing a period after the word *man.* Then verse eight begins with the verb *he humbled.* There are several peculiarities in such punctuation. First, the verb, as the first word in the new sentence, is without a connective, *de, oun,* or *gar.* This may not be conclusive against the period, but it is at least quite unusual in Greek. Second, the "abrupt separation in a group of clauses which have a close logical historical coherence is improbable" (Ellicott, 58). And, third, the common translations, without a period, make perfectly good sense.

The word *schematized (schematī)* attracts attention. Is it simply a synonym of *omoiomati?* That there should be a repetition of the thought, with a different word, is not suspicious. Authors often use such an expedient. This then would be an emphasis on the unlikeness between Jesus and ordinary human persons. In fact, *schematī* stresses the dissimilarity more than the *omoiomatī* does.

Martin stresses the likeness rather than the unlikeness: "our Lord was truly Man and not only that he became like a man" (181). But we must insist that Christ was not a human person somehow associated with a divine person. As indicated in the preceding, we must avoid Nestorianism.* But we must also insist on human characteristics, and, in the following phrases, on corporeal characteristics, for the necessity of the incarnation lay in the possibility of death.

There is no disguising the fact that a correct statement describing the incarnate Son of God is hard to complete. It is easy enough to say that he took to himself a human body in order to die. It is easy also to recognize that Jesus' thoughts were often on a human level. The most conspicuous of these was his ignorance of the date of his return. Not so conspicuous but broader in scope is the assertion in Luke 2:52 that he not only increased in stature, but also "in wisdom and . . . in favor with God." The creeds and catechisms say that our Lord had a true body and a reasonable (rational) soul. But does not the assertion of a human soul imply Nestorianism? Note that the Westminster Confession says that the Son "did take upon him man's nature, with all the essential properties and common infirmities thereof . . . so that the whole, perfect, and distinct natures . . . were inseparably joined in one person . . . which person is very God and very man, yet one Christ." The Larger Catechism (Q. 9, 36, 37), after saying, "two entire distinct natures and one person forever," adds that he took "to himself a true body and a reasonable soul." But would not this mean that Christ had or was a human person? He now had a soul which he had not had before the incarnation. Does not this make him a human person? What is a soul, anyway? The Catechism, in defense of assigning to him a reasonable soul, quotes Matthew 26:38, "My soul is exceeding sorrowful, even unto death." Perhaps the Westminster theologians would be displeased by the suggestion tha the term *soul* in Matthew 26:38 is used colloquially rather than theologically and philosophically. But there is Scrip-

---

* Clark's remarks here and elsewhere in this book on Christ's person reflect his views during most of his life. During the last two years he changed his view on the person of Christ, and his later view may be found in *The Incarnation.*– Editor.

tural evidence for so suggesting. In Luke 12:19 the wealthy farmer said, "I will say to my soul, Soul, thou hast much goods laid up for many years; take thine ease, eat, drink, and be merry." Now, the fact that thinking is a function of the soul in its strict philosophical sense cannot be denied; but one must also note that the farmer aimed at ease, eating, and drinking. These are bodily, not spiritual, functions; and hence the term *soul* as used here is more extensive than, and inconsistent with, its philosophical usage.

One may note that Charles Hodge (*Systematic Theology*, II, 385) attempts an explanation of Philippians 2:6-11. He rejects the idea that *morphē* is synonymous with *phusis*. He asserts, though the assertion seems doubtful, that "No one can appear or exist in the view of others in the form of God, i.e. manifesting all divine perfections, who is not God." This is doubtful because, first, even Jesus did not manifest to the public all divine perfections; and, second, others who claimed to be the Messiah appeared to some deluded onlookers as divine. A page or so later Hodge has a section on "The Hypostatical Union." He depends mainly on (1) his personal intuition, which many people do not share; and (2) the Aristotelian concept of substance, which has a less than substantial justification.

I am only too well aware that this discussion has been seriously incomplete. But it must end by saying that Nestorianism faces worse difficulties, and that the liberal views of men like A. B. Bruce, *The Humiliation of Christ*, a masterful 450 page treatise, cannot be accepted as orthodox accounts of the Biblical material.

The next phrase is, "he humbled himself." What this humiliation consisted of, or at least what the final and extreme form of this humiliation was, the text immediately states: "becoming obedient even to death, indeed, death on a cross." There is a consistency here between the form of a slave and death on a cross. Roman citizens, if convicted of a capital offense, were beheaded; slaves were crucified. The literary emphasis falls on the final word, *cross*.

Not only was the physical death something terrible and indescribably cruel; not only was it a disgrace worse than all others; but in the eyes of the Jews it was a curse from God. However much we abhor the Pharisees, we cannot deny that to the Jews the crucifixion was proof that Christ's claims were false. Indeed, in another sense also, it was a curse from God. Jesus bore the curse and punishment due to us for our sins. But how could a Jew accept this idea in the light of the Old Testament that seemed to say that no one crucified could ever be received in Heaven? After two thousand years of Christian education, we are likely to forget, or at least to minimize, the Jewish reluctance to accept Jesus as their Messiah.

The idea that the Son of God should voluntarily accept such a death is stupendous. That he needed an incarnation to do so is uncomplicatedly obvious. But it is impossible to agree with Luther's declaration, "If I permit myself to be persuaded that only the human nature has suffered for me, then Christ is to me a poor Savior, then he himself, indeed, needs a Savior." The last phrase is really ridiculous, for Christ was sinless, and suffering in his divine nature is not a necessary presupposition for sinlessness. But more profoundly, the divine nature is incapable of suffering. The Son had to become man in order to do what God could not do. Does this deny omnipotence? No; it asserts that Deity is naturally unchangeable, immutable, without bodily parts and without passions. The reason the Son assumed a human nature was that he could not suffer without it.

2:9   **Therefore God also [highly] exalted him and graciously favored him with the name that is above every name...**

The *therefore* refers to Christ's humiliation. Because of such humiliation God exalted him. But next there comes a difficulty. The text says *echarisato,* graciously favored, him. But how can this be a *gracious* favor, when Christ himself *merited* it? Several commentators correctly perceive that it was the Son's human nature which God exalted. The divine nature was eternally beyond exaltation. But few if any commentators notice the apparent incongruity of the idea of grace–unmerited favor. Christ's exaltation was not unmerited. Perhaps it might be said that Christ's perfectly sinless nature merited freedom from punishment for sin, but still did not merit a name that is above every name. This seems to me a somewhat dubious escape from the difficulty. The only other possibility, so far as I can see, is to weaken the meaning of *echarisato* and have it say, "Because of your humiliation, I, the Father, assign to you this name or honor." But this is dubious Greek.

A relatively minor point is that the exaltation is not the resurrection. It is an exaltation in dignity. Nor is it the ascension. It consists in giving Christ a name. Motyer identifies this name as *Lord.* But *Lord* is a title, not a name. What the name is, is clearly stated in the next verse.

Before we do the next verse, however, there is an historical note of moderate interest. Strange as it may seem, in fact virtually incredible, the Arians of the fourth century used these verses to disprove the Deity of Christ. Eusebius and Arius argued that if Christ were exalted to a higher position, he could not have been divine, for there is no further rank or exaltation possible for Deity. Conversely if someone receives any higher qualifications as a reward for something he did, he cannot have had those qualifications as an original natural endowment. Now, this is strange and virtually incredible, not because it is such an obvious misinterpretation of the verse in Philippians, but because the argument, even on Arian principles, backfires. The argument would imply that Christ could not even have been the first created angel. The only rank above the first created angel would be God himself; and it is self-contradictory to suppose that a created being could somehow be promoted to the rank of an uncreated being, a temporal being to the rank of an eternal being. Paul of Samosata could use the argument because he held that Christ was a mere man.

2:10 . . . **that in the name of Jesus every knee should bow, of those in Heaven and those on Earth and those under the Earth . . .**

After the word *knee* and before the word *tongue* in the next verse, it is strange that the King James and the Revised Version should speak of *things* rather than of persons. The American Revised Version has *those;* the Revised Standard Version and New International Version rather dodge the decision by saying "every knee in heaven" etc. but the genitive plural *(epouraniōn)* cannot be so translated.

That the blessed angels and redeemed humanity should so worship Jesus is not surprising, but some readers might not anticipate a similar posture by the reprobate and the fallen angels, including Satan himself. Nevertheless, it is so, though the former worship freely and gladly, while the latter are compelled by constraint.

2:11 . . . **and every tongue confess that Jesus Christ is Lord to the glory of God, Father.**

Perhaps it is not necessary to point out that the sequence of phrases is more literary than logical. Yet two or three commentators have failed to see what most readers, correctly, get without hardly a second thought. The final phrase, "to the glory of God, the Father" is not a part of the confession. A clearer order swould be, "every tongue shall confess, to the glory of God the Father, that Jesus Christ is Lord." Even the demons' compulsory acknowledgment will glorify the Father.

2:12 **Consequently, my beloved, as you have always obeyed, not as in my presence only but now all the more in my absence, with fear and trembling work out your own salvation . . .**

There are a few minor points which can be disposed of briefly.

Chapter Two

The word *consequently* is not the *therefore* of logical conclusion, but rather an introduction to an exhortation. The long clause, "not as in my presence . . . in my absence" cannot be attached to the preceding verb *obeyed*–that makes no sense at all–but with the following verb *work out*. Observe the word *now*. It emphasizes the exhortation.

More important are the words "your own salvation." Martin's view is most peculiar. He holds that the word *salvation* does not refer to an individual's regeneration, sanctification, and entrance into Heaven. He writes,

> The true exegesis must begin with a definition of *salvation*, not in personal terms, but in regard to the corporate life of the Philippian church. The readers are being encouraged to concentrate upon reforming their church life. . . . *Your own, heautōn,* can hardly be taken in a personal sense . . . since the apostle is urging the Philippians to have their eye fixed on the interest of others and not to be preoccupied with their own concerns. The reference here must look back to 1:28 where the salvation of the Christian community as a whole is in view (111).

Now, first, 1:28 and any other verses that might conduce to the peace of the congregation, envisage personal salvation, because considerate conduct among the communicant members is very much a matter of individual sanctification. Furthermore, if Paul had in mind the salvation of the congregation as such, he would have been prophesying its eternal security. But that congregation, as a unitary corporate body, long ago ceased to exist. Once more, *perdition* in 1:28, and even the frequently used verb *appolumi,* are not usually applied to congregations but to individuals. The term *apōleia* occurs about twenty times in the New Testament, and perhaps only once does not designate damnation. In the next chapter, 3:19, the meaning is clear.

The most important phrase for exegesis is, "work out your own salvation." And not only work it out, but work it out in fear and trembling. After all, we are saved by works and not by faith, are we not? Therefore we should tremble and be afraid lest we fall from our temporary state of peace and be finally lost. As Lenski says, "The danger for the saved is ever that they grow otiose, secure, and thus through their own fault lose the salvation bestowed on them by God" (798). Lenski is a good Lutheran.

The Arminians are worse than the Lutherans, on this point anyway. They hold that this verse militates against the doctrine of divine repobation and implies that man is active rather than passive in the most important spiritual matters: He exercises faith in Christ before regeneration, and if he should be passive in regeneration rather than synergistic, he can later frustrate the grace of God, lose his salvation, and if fortunate be regenerated several times more. Those who write on this verse are likely to say that the exhortation to work out one's salvation is incompatible with the Calvinistic doctrine of reprobation, which latter is a mockery of the Gospel. Anyone who so argues, be he Lutheran, Arminian, or speed reader, should note that this exhortation is not addressed to all men, and particularly not to reprobates. Paul addresses the saints in Jesus Christ with their bishops and deacons, in whom the work of grace has already begun, which work God will most certainly complete.

Of course some, even many, Arminians would agree that Paul here addresses Christians. Yet like Lenski they would still assert that the verse teaches the possibility of losing one's salvation. To which we reply that they have read only half of the sentence. The remainder of the sentence, to express it in chaste, academic language, packs a wallop.

2:13   . . . **for it is God who works in you, both to will and to do, of his good pleasure.**

The first word, the connective *for,* does not introduce a precise logical conclusion, as Eadie notes, but an explanatory statement to enforce the exhortation. If Paul's imprisonment had not utterly cast the Philippians into the depths of desair, surely it could not have had the effect cheerleaders aim at during a football game. Some of the Philippians must have been discouraged. But beyond the actual situation, worse times were to follow. Had the Philippians known what later emperors would do, they might well have been filled with fear and trembling. Yet even this may not have been uppermost in Paul's mind. Though Paul, and Peter as well, knew that persecution would occur, they also saw the dangers of false teachers and of the temptations of the devil. Hence the apostles recognized that encouragement was needed; and here Paul exhorts the Philippians to persevere, in confidence that God works in them both to will and to do, and that he will finish the good work he began.

The two *kai*'s contribute an emphasis. "Both . . . and" is stronger than "and" alone. The idea is that God not only gives us physical strength to engage in Christian activity, but he first controls our will so that as a result of his control we decide or will to do our duty. It is strange, it is incomprehensible, that some commentators use this verse to attack Calvinism: "the Calvinistic writers are exceedingly embarrassed with it." The gentleman mentions Doddridge, though how the verse can embarrass Calvinists remains unexplained. The verse is among the strongest supports for Calvinism. Nobody, at least I do not see how anybody, could miss the statement that God controls a man's will as well as his actions. Ellicott notes, "the *thelein* no less than the *energein* is a direct result of the divine *energeia*" (64, col. 2). This is correct, even though Ellicott then tries to avoid the full force of his own words.

The idea that man has free will, an idea sponsored by Pelagius, adapted by the Council of Trent, and emphasized by Arminius and Wesley, is totally inconsistent with the Biblical plan of salvation. It is also inconsistent with the sovereignty of God, with divine omniscience and omnipotence, with the necessity of regeneration by the Holy Spirit, and of course with the pervasive Scriptural teaching of predestination.*

The climax comes in the last word, *eudokias,* God's good pleasure. Translators do not all agree on how to render the preposition *uper* that governs *eudokia.* The King James says, "of his good pleasure." The New American Standard and Revised Standard Version have *for.* The New International Version dodges the difficulty.

The proposition *uper* has many meanings. It governs both the genitive and the accusative. Here it takes the former. It often means *for;* but note that the English *for* itself has several meanings. *Uper* can mean *instead of,* as when a stenographer types a letter for her boss and puts her initials at the bottom. Clearly the context here does not permit it to mean "instead of his good pleasure." The Arndt and Gingrich lexicon has a good two columns on *uper* with the genitive. Liddell and Scott has over 100 lines of fine print on *uper* with the genitive: *over, above, beyond, on behalf of, by reason of, for the purpose of, on account of,* and *concerning.*

Now, although the sense prohibits the translation *instead of,* we could since the letter is typed by the stenographer as well as *instead of* the boss, translate the verse as "God works in us to will by his good pleasure."

The choice of a translation must depend on the context. For example, John 11:4 says, "This sickness is not unto death, but *uper* [on account of] the glory of God." That is to say, God ordained Lazarus' sickness, by which he died, in order to glorify the Son. God caused Lazarus' death because it pleased him to do so. Hebrews 5:1 is a good example of the necessity of a context. It reads. "Every high priest is ordained *uper* men . . . in order to bring gifts and sacrifices *uper* sins." The first *uper* means *on be-*

---

* How pervasive, I have tried to show in *Biblical Predestination,* Presbyterian and Reformed Publishing Co., 1969; and *Predestination in the Old Testament,* 1978. This latter was a response to an incredibly perverse account of the Old Testament. (Both books have been issued in a combined edition, *Predestination.–Editor.*)

half of, for the good of, for the benefit of; the second *uper* cannot possibly have the same meaning. In a very real sense, the sacrifices and therefore the ordination were caused by sin. Had there been no sin, there would have been no propitiatory sacrifices. The Textus Receptus has *uper* at the end of verse 3 also. Although *on behalf of* is probably the most frequent meaning, the *uper* in Luke 9:50 is rather different. The first *uper* in 1 Corinthians 4:6 cannot mean *on behalf of,* though the second probably does. In 1 Corinthians 10:30 *on behalf of* is impossible: *on account of* or *because of,* is required. Now, this list of instances, though very incomplete, may have bored the ordinary reader. Nevertheless an important point has been made. Whatever the New American Standard and Revised Standard Version mean by their word *for,* and their meaning is not at all clear, the translation *because of* cannot be rejected on any lexical grounds. The context permits, indeed the context requires the translation, "God works in us both to will and to do *because of, on account of,* or *by* his good pleasure."

There is more to say on these two verses, for as yet "fear and trembling" has not been explained. Those who hold that regeneration is a result of humanly initiated faith and must be protected by further good works see in this fear a fear of eternal punishment and because of that fear they must tremble. If the state of regeneration were permanent, and if one could not possibly fall from grace, and if God were really going to complete his good work in us, there would be no place for fear. This Romish, Lutheran, Arminian position fails to take into account the fact that there are different objects of fear. Beautiful ladies are supposed to be afraid of mice; muscular lumberjacks are understandably afraid of moose, rattlesnakes, and grizzlies. What then is the object of fear in these verses? To begin with, is it plausible that Paul is warning the Philippians to fear damnation when he himself was confident (1:6 says *confident* or *being persuaded)* that God would complete the work he had begun? Notice that in some instances the antonym of fear is pride. Proverbs 23:17 speaks of fear as reverence or submission. Proverbs 28:4 contrasts fear with the hardening of the heart. Hebrews 12:28 speaks of reverence and godly fear. In 1 Peter 1:17 fear is virtually gratitude and awe. Jeremiah 32:40 says, "I will put my fear in their hearts that they shall not depart from me." The fear itself is a basis of assurance and confidence. Does this not cover the Arminians with shame?

It must also be noted that *salvation* has several aspects. Some people say, "I was saved on December 31 at 6:05 p.m." If the statement is true, it can mean only that they were regenerated at that time. But sanctification and eventually glorification are also parts of salvation. Therefore when Paul says, "Work out your own salvation," thereby indicating a process, he is referring to sanctification and not to regeneration. Once again this ties in with God's beginning a work that proceeds go to completion. In this process, as is absolutely not the case in regeneration or justification, we have some work to do. And God works in us, not only to do such work, but beforehand to will to do such work.

The Romish-Arminian position is fundamentally based, not on exegesis of Scripture, but on certain assumptions in secular philosophy. One assumption is that moral responsibility is inconsistent with divine sovereignty. Rather than going too deeply into ethical theory, we may repeat an illustration that they frequently use. Calvinistic determinism, they say, pictures man as a mere robot. But if those who deserted the principles of the Reformation and took five theological steps back toward Romanism in the early seventeenth century can use a secular illustration, we who remained true to Calvin and Knox and those who formulated the Westminster Confession about twenty-five years later surely have the right to use a Biblical illustration. Both the Old Testament and the New picture God as a potter who forms and breaks men like non-resisting clay. Isaiah acknowledged (64:8), "Now, O Lord, . . . we are the clay and thou art our potter." Jeremiah 18:6 says, "Cannot I do with you as this potter . . . as the clay is in the potter's hand, so are ye in my hand." "Shall the clay say to him that fashioneth it, What makest thou?" (Isaiah 45:9). I might also quote Romans 9:21-24, but the critical edition of the Arminian Bible has deleted the whole chapter. The robot or puppet illustration suffers, not because it is deterministic, but because it is not deterministic enough. An operator cannot completely control a puppet. It places limitations on him. But God is omnipotent, and man is unable to place any limitation on him. The Bible compares man with clay which the Potter can fashion in any shape he wishes.

In addition to illustrations, the underlying secular philosophy of the Arminians assumes that determinism is inconsistent with moral responsibility. Actually moral responsibility is inconsistent with free will, because the latter makes rational choice impossible, and the resulting insanity destroys responsibility.*

If the reader thinks this material too philosophical and wants to get back to the more elementary exegesis, there is at least one further Scriptural teaching that needs mention. Although one man cannot control another's will, though he may sometimes force external compliance or even destroy his personality, the relation between man and God is quite different. Not only is God omnipotent in controlling men's overt actions, but he also has access to man's intellect and will. He can make a man think any thoughts he wants him to think. Note that God caused Absalom to think foolish thoughts so as to bring evil upon Absalom (2 Samuel 17:14). Predestinating omnipotence is a sufficient explanation for this control of human thought. But the apostle Paul expresses by a more fundamental detail *how* God's mind and ours are so closely related. It is not that God dwells in us, but rather that we live and move and have our being in God. This is also the basis for a Christian epistemology; but now we really must get back to the more superficial exegesis.

2:14, 15, 16 Do all things without grumbling or bickering, in order that you may be blameless and

---

* See my "Determinism and Responsibility," *The Evangelical Quarterly,* January 1932.

> sincere, children of God, without blemish in the midst of a crooked and twisted generation, among whom you appear as luminaries in the world, holding forth the word of life, so that I may boast in the day of Christ, because I did not run in vain nor did I labor in vain.

The exegesis of these verses is so superficial that it hardly seems needed. There are, however, some minor remarks that can be made.

The term *grumbling* seems to have God as its object, as it does in 1 Peter 4:9. This is supported by the Old Testament background in Deuteronomy 32:5, quoted in Psalm 78:8, from which Paul takes the words "perverse and crooked generation." The term *dialogismōn,* however, would ordinarily refer to human disputants, though of course some men have remonstrated with God. Perhaps my translation *bickering* humanizes the verse too much. In the next phrase *sincere* is better than *harmless,* possibly because bickering with God is very apt to be insincere.

The word *appear* in the phrase, "among whom you appear as luminaries in the world," presents a slight difficulty. It seems rather false than true that the Christians appeared to the Romans as divinely ordained luminaries. Lucian degrades them by castigating together Epicureans, atheists, and Christians. The difficulty is avoided by noting that the text does not identify those to whom the Christians appear as lights in the world. Remember that Christ said, not that you *shall be* the light of the world, but that you *are;* and surely this did not appear so to the general public. We may regard the general public as blind, in which case the Christians appear to God as light in the darkness. Lenski avoids the difficulty *ab initio* by translating the verb as *shine,* rather than as *appear;* but the lexicons give virtually no support for assigning an active meaning to a middle form.

Another relatively unimportant point is whether the Philippians held onto the word of life or whether they held it forth in their evangelistic endeavors. This merges into the question whether the word of life is the Gospel or whether it is the Word, Christ. If they held forth, the word is the Gospel; if they held to the word, the word could be either Christ himself or the good news which they held by believing. New Testament usage seems to favor hold forth. To hold onto Christ, or even holding onto the Gospel, would have probably taken the verb *katechō* instead of *epechō,* as in 1 Corinthians 11:2 and 15:2; 2 Corinthians 6:10, and 1 Thessalonians 5:21. There are five instances of *epechō* in the New Testament, and the other four more readily mean *hold forth* than hold tight. Müller agrees; Motyer wants it both ways; Lenski disagrees. It seems to me that in contrast with Lenski, Eadie had pretty well settled the question (142-144).

The last two lines of these three verses belong logically, not grammatically, to the next two of the paragraph.

2:16, 17, 18 . . . so that I may boast in the day of Christ because I did not run in vain nor did I labor in vain; but even if I am poured out upon the sacrifice and worship of your faith, I rejoice– with you all; the same also you rejoice and rejoice–with me.

Paul was understandably concerned that his life-work should not be a failure. At that great day he wanted to say, "I have fought a good fight." This is true even if he should be immediately executed, a thought which he expresses in highly metaphorical language. He pictures an altar on which the faith of the Philippians is placed as a sacrifice, and on this sacrifice Paul's blood is poured as a libation. However dismal and macabre the metaphor is, Paul is not dismayed by the prospect of martyrdom. He can rejoice alone, and he wants the Philippians to rejoice with him, for he knows that he has indeed not run in vain.

Several commentators note that in Jewish sacrifices the libation was poured out on the ground, while in heathen sacrifices it was poured on the victim. This is utterly unimportant, though two things might occur to a curious reader: First, Paul's martyrdom, even if pictured as a sacrifice of the Philippians' faith, would indeed be a heathen sacrifice; second, the preposition *epi* (upon) can be taken a little vaguely, as "upon the occasion of," or even "in addition to." The matter is trivial. Metaphors are hardly ever exact. Lenski discusses a few more trivialities. His attempt to take *spendomai* (pour) as middle, "I pour myself out," instead of passive, "I am poured out," seems perverse. Paul was not contemplating suicide. My very crabbed translation, "the same also," obviously means "for the same reason you also should rejoice."

2:19 **I hope in [the] Lord Jesus quickly to send Timothy to you, in order that I also may take heart when I learn of your affairs.**

Sometimes it is more difficult to make a crabbed translation than one in better style. The first verb is easy enough: It means *hope* and not *trust*. The one Greek word, "may take heart," an hapaxlegomenon in the New Testament, seems to have no literal equivalent in English. It could be "that I become good-souled." If it were further necessary to explain that the metaphorical sacrifice was not a divine prediction of his immediate execution, one could note that here Paul hopes not only to send Timothy to Philippi, but also hopes to live until he returns to Rome, or at least until Timothy returns.

A more interesting point is the preposition before the word *Lord*. Few commentators, so it seems, realize how frequently the Greek preposition *en* does not mean *in*. Here as in many places the local meaning of *en* is simply impossible. Devotional writers often drool about being *in* Christ. Particularly when Paul says, "In him we live and move and have our being," there can be no thought of any spatial inclusion. Hence there is at least the possibility that here too a better translation can be found. Why not "I hope by the Lord to send Timothy..."? Remember that James 4:13-15 says,

"Go to now, ye that say, Today or tomorrow we will go . . . buy and sell and get gain: whereas ye know not what shall be on the morrow. . . . For ye ought to say, if the Lord will, we shall live and do this or that." Then why cannot Paul have thought and said, "I hope that by the decree of the Lord I can send Timothy"?

2:20, 21 For I have no equal-soul who will genuinely care for your affairs, for they all seek their own [advantage], not that of Jesus Christ.

"Equal-soul" *(isopsuchon)* is another hapaxlegomenon. Two of them in successive verses. This may indicate that Paul is emphatic. The New English Bible has, "No one else here who sees things as I do." Müller does not like this and insists that *autō,* not *moi,* must be inserted: like *him,* not like *me.* But that is the trouble: How can we decide which absent word to insert into the text? Either one makes tolerable sense. The difficulty is that there is really a double comparison. Timothy is better than the others, for the others have several faults, as the next verse says. But Timothy's freedom from those faults depends on his like-mindedness with Paul.

Unlike Timothy all the others seek their own advantage. This condemnatory judgment allows for no exception. We must remember, however, that Luke and Aristarchus were no longer in Rome. We must assume also that the sincere evangelists of 1:1 had left. Recall that in 2 Timothy 4:16 Paul says, "At my first defense no one stayed with me, but all deserted me." Martin makes the incredible suggestions that the words "all seek their own advantage" are a parenthetical aside which refers to the pagan world as a whole and does not refer to any Christian.

2:22, 23, 24 But you know his reputation, that as a boy [serves] his father, he served me toward [advancing] the Gospel. Accordingly I hope to send this man immediately as soon as I see

> what concerns me; and I am persuaded by the Lord that even I myself shall soon come.

The commentaries generally have little to say on these three verses because there is little that needs explanation. The only two points in doubt are (1) the outcome of Paul's trial, and (2) the order in which two of these men visited the Philippian church.

First, although Paul speaks hesitantly, or at least without presumption, it seems likely that the Lord had persuaded him by a revelation that he would be acquitted. Second, Epaphroditus, as we shall see in the next verse, had already been sent to Philippi. His absence was one factor in making verse 21 possible. As for Timothy, Paul intended to send him immediately *(exautēs)*. Perhaps he carried this letter with him. Then quickly after *(tacheōs)* the acquittal, Paul would follow.

2:25 > **But I thought it necessary to send to you Epaphroditus, my brother and co-worker and fellow-soldier, but your apostle, and minister of my need...**

The first verb, *thought,* aorist tense, shows that the New International Version translation, "I think," is incorrect. The New International Version implies that Epaphroditus was still in Rome and therefore Paul's denunciation in verse 21 applies to him along with the others. The Revised Standard Version has an ambiguous perfect tense. It suggests, though not emphatically, that Epaphroditus was still in Rome. The American Standard Version, as usually, is correct. Several commentators insist that the verb is an "epistolary" aorist; that is to say, Paul imagines himself in Philippi at the time the letter is received there and hence can look back and say, "I thought"; but in Rome Paul's thinking was present, not past. This is an assertion, but no reason is given why it must be so regarded. Though epistolary aorists are quite possible, what tense but the aorist could Paul have used if he wished to say, "I thought" at a time prior to writing this letter? Lenski, however, believes that Epaphroditus was still in Rome, on the ground that verse 29 tells the Philippians to receive him when he comes. But this request would be impossible if Epaphroditus had arrived before Paul's letter. Lenski argues, "Paul could get no one else to go to Philippi. . . . How did Paul then send his present letter? By some stranger? Epaphroditus is to be the bearer. . . . vv. 19-23 show that Paul has no other man to take his present letter to Philippi" (818). Lenski's difficulties, however, seem to disappear when we recall that Paul had just said he would send Timothy immediately.

Next, some readers may find it strange that Epaphroditus is called an *apostle*. Were there not thirteen apostles only? Of course the commentators usually remark that here the word *apostle* is not used in its technical and official sense. Some translations use the word *messenger* or *commissioner*. Can this be substantiated by the text? Motyer and Eadie sort of stumble on the explanation without seeming to realize it. Most are content with the bare assertion. The explanation, as I see it, lies in the genitive pronoun *your*, somewhat emphasized by the preceding pronoun *my*. An apostle in the official sense is a man whom God has sent, particularly a man who saw Christ after his resurrection. Epaphroditus is a man whom you–the Philippians–have sent. The Philippians had sent Epaphroditus to minister to Paul. He had brought needed money to Paul, a contribution from the Philippians, but, at least equally important, also personal service. His personal service, however, was unfortunately interrupted, as the next two verses show.

2:26, 27 **... since he was longing for you all, and was distressed because you heard that he was sick. Indeed he was sick near to death; but God had mercy on him, and not on him only, but also on me, that I should not have pain upon pain.**

Paul does not describe the situation in all its details. Some points are clear enough and we need not, like Hendriksen, invent two or three pages of mere imagination.

The verse seems to support the idea that Paul had already sent Epaphroditus back to Philippi. He had come to help Paul. He had fallen seriously ill. The Philippians had heard of his illness and they were worried. This worried Epaphroditus. He recovered. Paul sent him back because Epaphroditus longed for them. Maybe also Paul wanted the Philippians to see that their messenger was now well and strong.

The phrase *pain upon pain,* or sorrow upon sorrow, is no exaggeration. Paul's imprisonment was one, Epaphroditus' illness was another, and his death would have been worse; and then neither man wanted the Philippians to be upset; and not only upset but perhaps they faced more external and internal difficulties than they would have faced if their officials could have been there.

All these details, however, are relatively trivial. The Scriptures are true and useful throughout, but not every verse is of the same degree of importance. Here are good examples to follow if we find ourselves in similar circumstances; but few of us do. In times of persecution passages such as this one would be more useful. The political liberals, the abortionists, the homosexuals are trying to reduce Bible-believers to the status of second rate citizenship. They object when we are vocal about crime and corruption in the bureaucracies. Persecution may yet come. But we do not face it now.

2:28, 29, 30 More urgently then I sent him that seeing him again you might be glad and I less sorrowful. Receive him therefore in the Lord with all joy and hold such men in high regard, for he nearly died through his work for Christ, risking his soul that he might make up for your inability to serve me.

"**More urgently**" **indicates that** Paul had for some time intended to send Epaphroditus, but when he learned how disturbed the Philippians were, he sent him off pronto.

As for the risks Epaphroditus had run, and his serious illness, one can only guess. Travel itself was risky. There must have been many ships that sank in those days. Travel on land was both laborious and dangerous. Then, too, even if Paul was about to be acquitted, Rome was a dangerous place for any Christian. What other risks Epaphroditus ran, we do not know.

The final phrase is worse in English than in Greek: the King James says, "your lack of service"; the New American Standard has "what was deficient in your service"; for once the New International Version is much better, "the help you could not give me." Paul was not scolding the Philippians; he merely referred to the obvious fact that the Philippians could not take care of all his needs. What they could not do in person, Epaphroditus did for them.

Aside from these few remarks, and also aside from one or two textual trivialities, these verses need no commentary at all.

CHAPTER THREE

3:1   **For the rest, my brethren, rejoice in the Lord. To write the same things to you is no trouble for me, but for you it is safe.**

The words "For the rest" or "finally" sound as if Paul were ending the letter. In fact, the word translated *rejoice* also means fare-well. But the actual conclusion is delayed to 4:8; at least that verse repeats "Finally." Even there the conclusion is long enough. Lenski argues that *to loipon* does not particularly mean finally: It is a sequential *furthermore,* of which several can occur in a letter. On the whole it is not likely that Paul intended to close the letter here, for the remainder of the letter is almost as long as what precedes.

What does Paul mean by "the same thing"? One answer is: all the two preceding chapters. But this cannot possibly be the case. Lenski for no obvious reason specifies 1:27, 30. One must judge whether the remainder of the third chapter is "the same thing" as the brief mention of adversaries in 1:28. A more reasonable suggestion, though it is only a guess, is that Paul here repeats what he had said in previous letters (now lost) to the Philippians. Polycarp asserts that he had written several. Perhaps the best suggestion is that he is reminding the Philippians of things he had told them when he was there. A great deal of ingenuity has been wasted on those few words.

The word *safe* in the phrase "For you it is safe" is also peculiar. The meaning, however, is clear enough and can be more fully expressed by saying, "a repetition of my instructions with reference to heretical enemies will help you to deal safely or more effectively with them." The next verse bears this out.

3:2 **Beware of the dogs, beware of those who do evil, beware of the mutilation.**

This three-fold denunciation is not directed against three different groups of people; in particular it is not directed against the jealous preachers mentioned in 1:15-18. The present warning refers to Judaizers, as the next few verses make clear. That these Jewish pseudo-Christians were a great danger to and in the church can be understood from the epistle to the Galatians and from the Pastoral epistles. 1 Timothy 1:4, 9; and Titus 2:14, 3:9 show that the Judaizers were dangerous, though this is not the main message of the Pastorals. Galatians, however, is mainly directed against them. Unlike the contemporary distaste for polemics, Paul speaks very harshly. Here he calls the Judaizers *dogs*–the modern equivalent would be scavengers–*evildoers* is literal and somewhat bland; but the term *mutilation* is cutting sarcasm. Paul is not here exercised over Jews who, either in ignorance of the Gospel, or in opposition to the Gospel, retain their traditional reverence for circumcision. His opponents are Jews who have made a profession of faith in Christ and yet insist that circumcision is necessary for salvation. Two considerations, in different ways, illustrate the danger. First, the psychological pressure of tradition is evident in the fact that Peter and Barnabas–incredibly–Peter and Barnabas succumbed to this false and anti-Christian view. Second, the view is anti-Christian because it nullifies Christ's atonement. Note that the Judaizers believed in Christ as Messiah; presumably they believed in the Virgin Birth; they acknowledged that Christ wrought miracles; that his death was a sacrifice; and that he rose from the dead. Yet Paul denounced them in the harshest terms. Why?

The answer is perfectly clear. They believed that something further was necessary to salvation. They believed that Christ's death was *necessary,* but they did not believe that his death was *sufficient.* Said Paul, "I testify again to every man that is circumcised that he is a debtor to do the whole law. Christ is become of no effect unto you" (Galatians 5:3,4). On such people Paul pronounced anathemas. He called them dogs. In using the term *katatōmen* he compared mutilation with *peritomē*, strongly suggesting that the circumcision of the Judaizers was the equivalent of heathen cuttings and self-mutilations.

The heathen practice of cutting oneself with knives is no longer a problem for the Christian church, unless the practice lingers on in some remote savage tribe. But the practice of trusting something else in addition to belief in Christ is with us still. Some people, besides Roman Catholics, believe in baptismal regeneration. Romanists often depend on the merits of the saints, the worship of Mary, not to mention their own good works. Today the Pope was welcomed in England where Bloody Mary burned Ridley, Latimer, and Cranmer at the stake, and where a later pope supported another Mary in an attempt to assassinate Elizabeth. Feeble demonstrations again the Pope in 1982 show that some few still are true to Paul's principles, but England isn't.

3:3, 4   **For we are the circumcision who worship the Spirit of God and boast in Christ Jesus and do not trust in the flesh, though I myself have trust even in the flesh. If any other seems to trust in the flesh, I more.**

There is a small textual, but greater grammatical or exegetical problem here. After saying that Christians are the true circumcision, the true subjects of the covenant, Paul describes this true circumcision as those who worship the Spirit of God. The word *God* is genitive. Another reading has *God* in the dative. In this case the translation would be, "those who worship God in spirit," and in truth as John 4:23 says. But though this reading avoids all difficulty in translation, for *latreuō* regularly takes the dative, the textual evidence greatly favors *theou, God* in the genitive. *Spirit* is dative, and hence we must translate it "we who worship the

Spirit of God." The New International Version says, "we who worship by the Spirit of God;" but there is no preposition in the text. For some strange reason the Revised Standard Version makes *theou* (or *theō*?) the object of the participle. Although the present writer does not favor blind obedience to Wescott and Hort or to Aland, Black, Metzger, and Wikgren, their reading in this case seems correct. At least no one can confidently assert that *theō* is original.

But then, is it not very peculiar to say "We who worship the Spirit of God"? Peculiar, yes; but not incorrect, for we worshp the Trinity, all three, and we use the apostolic benediction.

Worshiping the Spirit and boasting in Christ–*glorying* in Christ sounds better in English–excludes trusting or having confidence in the flesh. This phrase adds to the previous point that neither circumcision nor any other human work can save us. But what is this? Paul immediately begins to boast in the flesh!

Ordinarily in Greek the first person pronoun is not used. *Eimi,* am, means I am. This is true of the third person also: *esti,* is, means he, she, or it is. *Pisteuō,* one word, means I believe. But here Paul inserts the rare *egō:* "I myself," emphatic. Then immediately Paul adds further emphasis: If anyone else seems to have reason to trust in the flesh. I have much more. Paradoxical, no?

Well, yes, and so indicated. The phrase begins with *kaiper*–its only instance in the Pauline epistles. The grammarians call it a concessive conjunction. Let us put it this way: Paul boasts in Crhist although he has more reason to boast in his Jewish heritage than the Judaizers have. Paul is not ashamed of his Jewish background nor does he regard it as spiritually useless. In Romans 3:1 he asked, "what advantage then hath the Jew, or what profit is there of circumcision?" And instead of answering, None, he asserts, "Much every way." Also in 1 Timothy 1:8 he says, "The Law is good if a man use it lawfully."

In his present situation, confronting the Judaizers, Paul had to anticipate an accusation of belitting Jewish privileges because he himself had little claim to them. On the contrary he had a better claim than any of the Judaizers. The claim comes with crushing force in the next few verses. This line of argument does not negate the Gospel; it is concessive and negates salvation by works.

> **3:5, 6** **With respect to circumcision–the eighth day; of the race of Israel–the tribe of Benjamin, a Hebrew of the Hebrews; as to the Law–a Pharisee; as to zeal–persecuting the church; as to the righteousness which comes by the Law–blameless.**

That this is an overwhelming claim to superior social rank, anyone can see. Many commentators remark that the first King of Israel came from the tribe of Benjamin and that his name was Saul. That the tribe was loyal to David when the north seceded is to its honor, but King Saul was not a man of whom many would be proud. Whether some of the Judaizers were Greek-speaking Jews of the dispersion or not (probably some were), Paul was not a Hellenistic Jew. His parents, even in Tarsus, spoke Hebrew (or Aramaic). And while Paul does not mention his education under Gamaliel in Jerusalem, he pointedly tells us that he was a super-duper Pharisee. This exceptional devotion and zeal he demonstrated by actively persecuting the Christians. All of which supports his claim to having been blameless before the Law. Really, this is quite impressive.

> **3:7, 8** **But whatever things were gain to me, these I have considered loss because of Christ. But moreover indeed also I consider all things to be loss because of the superiority of the knowledge of Christ Jesus my Lord, by whom I lost all things, and I consider [them] garbage [or, excrement] that I may gain Christ . . .**

The verb *consider* occurs three times in these two verses. The change in tense is a matter of moderate interest. The first instance is perfect, "I have considered" with the common Greek implication that I still consider it so. The second instance is the simple present, "I consider" right now that all these things are useless. The third instance is also present: "I consider them [now] as garbage." There is another verb, "by whom I lost all [these] things." It is aorist tense, designating a single point or action in the past.

On the road to Damascus Paul came to know that Christ was the Messiah and the Son of God. This knowledge is superior to any knowledge of the Law, even to a correct understanding of the Law, let alone the incorrect Pharisaic interpretation. Although Paul often refers to Christ as Lord in a certain routine or common way, one wonders, because of the aorist tense, "by whom I lost all these things" whether or not Paul here had his conversion experience particularly in mind: "Who art thou, Lord?"

The phrase, "the superiority of the knowledge of Christ," seems to need a bit of explanation. It can hardly refer to the knowledge that Christ knows. It is clearly a knowledge that Paul has acquired. Presumably the main comparison is Paul's new knowledge about Christ versus the mistaken opinions of the Pharisees as to the nature of the expected Messiah and also as to the correct understanding of the Law. Paul very suddenly was given knowledge of the identity of the Messiah; but one should not imagine that he immediately acquired all the knowledge he later wrote down in his epistles. Remember that after his conversion on the road, and his public confession in Damacus, Paul retired into the wilderness for approximately three years. He did not immediately begin his missionary endeavors. The most reasonable suggestion is that it took him that long to reconstruct his understanding of the Old Testament and to develop its implications, which then he was able to preach and write in his epistles.

3:9   ... and that I may be found in him, not having my own righteousness, that by the Law,

> **but that through faith in Christ, the righteousness of God upon faith . . .**

American public schools have so corrupted the language of the country that all Christian college students, nearly all seminary students, and most ministers would translate the last two verbs as "that I might gain Christ and that I might be found. . . ." Between you and I, man, that ain't good English, y'know. Even punctuation makes a difference. Tischendorf has no comma between *him* and *not having*. This permits one to translate it as, "that I may be found by Christ not to have my own righteousness." This is a very good interpretation, but the American reader must remember that the Greek manuscripts have no puncutation at all–except an occasional period at the end of a long section. This is true of secular manuscripts as well as of the New Testament. In nineteen long lines of Aristotle's *Constitution of Athens,* copied in the first century, I cannot see, even with a magnifying glass, more than one period, if the thing is a period at all and not just an ink blot. The uncial Vaticanus of 2 Corinthians 3:1-4:6 seems to have one semi-colon, but I am not sure. Sometimes a blank space is left to indicate a break. Strange as it may seem, the papyri often have more punctuation than the uncials. We return to the exegesis, remembering that punctuation is a part of it.

Meyer very much objects to omitting the comma. He wants Christ to find Paul not having Paul's own righteousness. Meyer reasons that the omission of the comma is inconsistent with the *autō* (him) in the dative. This is a poor reason, for *autō* by this omission does not become superfluous. It is not superfluous because "by him" can refer to the day of judgment when Christ will find, or judically declare, that Paul's righteousness is the righteousness that comes through faith. This is a serious interpretation, but it is not for that reason correct. Meyer may be too anxious to preserve the comma; nevertheless, the comma seems justified, making the phrase somewhat independent of the preceding phrase. Paul will be found to be in Christ, and he will also be found to have the righteousness of faith.

There is a peculiar change of prepositions in the next line: "but that *dia* [by means of] faith in Christ, the righteousness of God *epi* upon the faith." At first sight *dia* seems to teach the Reformed doctrine of justification by means of faith, while *epi* seems to teach the Arminian doctrine of justification on the basis of faith. Calvinism teaches that the *basis* of justification is the righteousness of Christ, as chiefly exemplified in his sinless life and vicarious atonement. But how could a man of Paul's academic ability contradict himself in a single line? One is not so surprised that Ellicott can contradict himself in two sentences some twenty-seven lines apart (85). Near the top of the column he says, " 'that [righteousness] which is through faith in Christ;' of which faith in Christ is the *causa medians*." But below he continues, " 'based on faith' . . . *pistis* being the foundation on which it [righteousness] firmly and solidly rests." Martin also (148) says, *"epi tē pistei,* i.e. on the basis of human response to the offer of the gospel," thus leaving the merits of Christ in limbo. Hendriksen definitely mentions the imputation of Christ's righteousness, but he does not address the present problem. Motyer is likewise unclear. In a footnote Müller (114) says, *"Dia pisteos* denotes faith as a means, not as the ground or cause working the righteousness." Good enough; but he does not mention the following *epi.*

The answer to this puzzle comes in two parts, the first grammatical, the second theological. So far as grammar is concerned, *epi* with the dative frequently denotes the cause.

But even in classical Greek it does not always denote the cause. For example, Plato's *Apology,* 29, c, says, "We will acquit you on this condition, on the condition that you no longer . . . study philosophy." This is hardly causality. The cause would have been the reluctance of the judges to execute a man so well advanced in years.

There are also other uses of *epi* with the dative that are impossible here. For example, there is a metaphorical local sense, as in Matthew 24:47, "ruler over all his goods." Arndt and Gingrich gives a long list before it ever gets to the causal examples. Then too, Blass and Debrunner state, "*Epi* with dative. (1) The genitive and accusative predominate in the local sense, but a sharp division between them and the dative cannot be carried through." Later in the chapter, 3:12, *eph'ō* can hardly means *on the basis of which*. See the exegesis below.

To sum up the grammatical question, one may argue that if classical Greek shows some flexibility, hellenistic Greek allows for more, and hence *epi* in 3:9 cannot be restricted to *on the basis of*.

The theological argument therefore is decisive. If God pronounces a sinner righteous, there must be a source of such righteousness. That source is not Paul, as he explicitly said in the second phrase of this very verse. Throughout his epistles, and most emphatically in Romans, Paul teaches the imputation of Christ's righteousness–so that God may be both just in himself while he is also the justifier of him who believes in Jesus.

3:10, 11 ... **so as to know him and the power of his resurrection and community of his sufferings, being conformed to his death, if somehow I should arrive at the resurrection the [one] from the dead.**

A textual problem: Nearly all manuscripts (chief exceptions are Aleph and B, though a third hand in Aleph follows the majority) have an article before *pathēmatōn* (sufferings). The critical editions omit it. The only reason I can see for omitting it is that all the cursives have it. Something similar, though perhaps with better reason–it could hardly be worse–occurs at the end of verse 11.

Having Christ's imputed righteousness, as in the preceding verse, is for the purpose of knowing Christ and the power of his resurrection. Several commentators insist that this power is not the power revealed in Christ's rising from the tomb, nor Christ's power in raising the dead at his return, though Paul mentions the future resurrection in the next verse, but the power Christ gives to Paul at the moment. Could it mean the power to endure the sufferings mentioned in the next phrase?

But in the sentence the knowledge of *him* precedes the knowledge of his *power.* Perhaps knowing him is defined by knowing his power and sufferings. In this case the expanded translation would be: knowing him, that is, knowing both his power and his sufferings. The final phrase of the verse, "being conformed to his death," supports such an interpretation. This explanation of what sort of knowledge is meant avoids less preferable surmises. Hendriksen says that Paul "refers to a knowledge not only of the *mind* but also of the *heart.*" Hendriksen (and Müller) are correct when they use the term *mind.* How else could anyone know anything without a mind? But when he says "also of the heart," he introduces a dualism that is utterly foreign to the Old Testament, and therefore to the New Testament also. Heart and mind are synonymous. People who assert a duality never explain what a non-mental knowledge could possibly be. If they reply that *knowledge* can be sexual intercourse, as indeed it is not only in Hebrew, but also in Greek and Latin, it proves only that they do not know what knowing is.

The idea that Paul had in common with Christ a good deal of suffering does not mean that Paul's sufferings were vicarious. See my commentary of Colossians 1:24, where the wording is more easily misunderstood than here. Both Paul and Jesus suffered, and both suffered a great deal. They had suffering in common. Nor does "being conformed to his death" mean that Paul will be crucified. As a Roman citizen Paul could not be legally crucified. Nor did he expect to be.

Verse 11 is completely parenthetical, for verse 12 continues the ideas of verse 10.

The words "If somehow" do not express any doubt on Paul's part that he will be raised from the dead. They express a doubt as to how he will arrive at that point: by execution, present or future, or by a more natural death, or even by Christ's return. Somehow he will get there.

Resurrection *(exanastasin)* is a peculiar word. Neither Paul, except here, nor any other New Testament writer uses this noun, though the verb occurs three times. It may be connected with the moderately emphatic article in the phrase "resurrection, the [one] from the dead."

One thing it does most surely not mean. Hendriksen strangely reduces the term *resurrection* from its literal meaning to a figurative meaning: "These words give expression to Paul's intense longing and striving *to be raised completely above sin and selfishness so that he can be a most effective agent for the salvation of men to the glory of God*" (ital. all his).

Very few commentaries seem to agree. The Right Reverend Charles J. Ellicott, Lord Bishop of Gloucester and Bristol (such a lovely Anglican title), produces a persuasive explanation: "*exanastasin* kīl. 'the resurrection from the dead;' i.e. as the context suggests, the *first* resurrection (Revelation 20:5), when at the Lord's coming the dead in him shall rise first (1 Thessalonians 4:16) [though the comparison in this reference is not pertiment]: compare Luke 20:35. The first resurrection will include only true believers and will apparently precede the second, that of non-believers and disbelievers, in point of time."

In this century J. Oliver Buswell, Jr., and no doubt some others too, called attention to the fact that Paul does not speak of the resurrection of the dead (anastasin tōn nekrōn, but of the resurrection, the one from [among] the dead. Dr. Buswell considered that this language implies that some of the dead will remain dead for a time. This is plausible, for no one, not even the reprobate, will fail of resurrection.

3:12 **Not that I already grasped [it] nor already have been made perfect, but I pursue if also I may grasp [it], for the reason that also I was grasped by Christ.**

Although it does not help in explaining verses 12-14, an historical event proves interesting. Philip Doddridge in 1755 preached a sermon on these three verses and for its conclusion wrote, "Arise, my soul, stretch every nerve." Doddridge obviously thought that Paul pressed with vigor on to grasp the crown in 3:14. If, however, this prize *(brabeion)* were the resurrection from among the dead, the verse would not make good sense. The initial phrase, "not that I already grasped it," is an elucidation designed to prevent the readers from misunderstanding the previous verses. But there was no possibility of their thinking that Paul had already risen from the dead. Such a disclaimer would have been ridiculous. It is true that the resurrection was the last thing mentioned in the previous verse. But it seems that Paul then suspected that someone might misunderstand verse 10: After all, verses 10 and 11 are both parts of the same sentence. Hence Paul simply refers to a part of that sentence.

Furthermore, the difficulty is not quite so sharp in Greek as it is in the King James version. King James repeats the verb *attain;* but the text has two different verbs. In 3:11 *attain* is *katantēsō*, to *reach* or to *arrive.* The second verb is *elabon,* to *receive,* to *grasp,* to *obtain.* The fact that the verbs are different helps to remove the difficulty by protecting the parenthetical character of verse 11.

The two words *eph ō,* translated as "for the reason that," or more simply and perhaps better by the one word *because,* are not too well done in the King James: "that for which." This idea seems to be, "I follow after in order to grasp the goal which Christ had in mind when Christ grasped me." This somewhat distorts the sense. For one thing the final verb in the King James is in the present tense; but in the text it is aorist, "I was grasped." Hence the meaning is better expressed in the translation above. This ties in with 1:6, now applied to Paul instead of to the Philippians. Paul now pursues the goal because Christ had earlier taken charge of him.

There is another important point in this verse, but since its development runs into the next two verses, let us go on.

3:13, 14 **Brethren I do not consider myself to have grasped [it]. But [note] one thing, forgetting the past, but stretching out toward the future, I pursue the goal for the prize of the upward call of God in Christ Jesus.**

The first phrase of these two verses is more emphatic in Greek than in English. To indicate the stress, one would have to say, "I myself do not consider myself. . . ." Could it be that some of the Philippians considered themselves as Paul did not? Hendriksen thinks so. On this assumption Paul wants them to note this one thing, namely, he does not make such a claim for himself. This interpretation, however, does not find much favor among the commentators. They generally take it, as the versions also do, as "This one thing I do." Of course, this makes very good sense too. But the other is not impossible, for Paul in these verses is defending himself against a misunderstanding.

Theological aberrations of the eighteenth century required, for rebuttal, a more frequent use of these verses than contemporary liberalism does. Our present troubles are worse. Even so, there are still some who hold that sinless perfection is possible in this life. One example was a gentleman whom I knew fairly well. Now, this man had a delightful personality. He was modest, he was pleasant, and no one could suspect him of hypocrisy. Yet in his calm quiet way he stated clearly, "I have not sinned in the last twenty-six years." Verbatim. This was standard Arminianism, and still is, though the Arminians seem not to stress it so much now. In any case it conflicts with the Scripture. Here we may argue that if Paul had not attained perfection, surely none of the Philippians had.

But here is not the only New Testament denial of perfectionism. Combine, if you will, the teaching of the following few passages. "Forgive us our debts" (Matthew 6:12). A sinless person could not pray the Lord's Prayer.

Romans 7:14-24, though their interpretation is disputed, refer to Paul after his conversion, and show that he is not free from sinning. James 3:2-4 teach the same lesson. When 1 John 1:8 says, "If we say we have no sin, we deceive ourselves," John is referring to Christians, not to the unregenerate. The Old Testament also agrees: "there is no man that sinneth not," even the Arminians (1 Kings 8:46). Then Ecclesiastes 7:20 says, "there is not a just man upon Earth that doeth good and sinneth not." This should pretty well refute Wesleyanism.

Something needs to be said about the prize toward which Paul is straining. There seems to be come confusion here. Lenski bluntly says, "He has already named this *brabeion* or prize in v. 11: 'may arrive at the raising up from the dead.'" But we saw that Paul had no need to tell them that he had not yet been raised from the dead. Rather the unattained goal is sinless perfection, the *teteleiōmai* of verse 12. The race is the process of sanctification. Yet the words of verse 14 seem so definitely to refer to the resurrection and Heaven beyond, that the reader is confused. This dual reference, however, admits of an easy harmonization. Sinless perfection, the aim of being totally pleasing to God, is attained only in Heaven.

The phrase, "the upward call of God in Christ Jesus," needs more application than explanation. The word "upward" could indicate either the source of the call–the call from above–or it could point out the direction the call requires. The application, however, refers to a fairly common religious idea that there are many ways to God, of which Christ may be one, but not necessarily the best way for all. It is a sort of bland theism, or deism, if you will, though the latter term is out of date and has inappropriate connotations. It is hard to characterize the age in which one lives, but probably this sort of non-descript religion was more popular in the thirties than in the eighties. At any rate, I have more respect for an orthodox Jew who hates Christ, than for Hocking *et al.* who treat him with polite condescension.

3:15, 16, 17 Let those of us who are perfect think this; and if you think something otherwise, even this God will reveal to you; except to what we have attained, march in the same [rule and think the same thing]. Be imitators of us, brethren, and watch those who so walk as you have an example [namely] us.

After Paul in verse 12 had denied that anyone is perfect, it seems strange that here he says "all of us who are perfect. . . ." Actually this apparent inconsistency is easily clarified. 1 Corinthians 2:6 refers to some Christians who were "perfect." Presumably what is meant here is the same, as is more clearly stated in 14:20. Unfortunately the English versions are not so clear as the Greek. A literal translation is, "Brethren, don't be childish in your minds . . . but be perfect in your minds." In the same vein Ephesians 4:13 says, "Until we all attain to the unity of the faith and of the knowledge of the Son of God, to the [status of] a perfect man, to the measure of the age of the fulness of Christ." The idea therefore is Christian intellectual maturity. Martin is clearly wrong when he says, "the use of the verb *phronein* shows that it was more than an intellectual difference; it betrayed a different outlook and affected the conduct of those whom Paul had in mind" (155). First, this is poor Greek: The verb *phronein* does not necessarily mean "more than an intellectual difference." See Arndt and Gingrich, and also refer to Philippians 1:7. Second, a different "outlook" is itself an intellectual difference and cannot form the contrast Martin makes. Naturally a mature person does not think like a child, and his different thoughts eventually result in different actions. Naturally a mature man does not shoot marbles or play hide and seek. The important factor is his thinking. The supporting verses quoted just above should be sufficient to make this perfectly plain. Hence the difficulty in 3:15 is removed.

Supporting the intellectual interpretation of this phrase, the last phrase of the verse says, "God will reveal this to you." Now, revelation is directed to man's intellect. Much of it, such as the doctrine of the Deity of Christ, or the federal headship of Adam, gives no directions for conduct; and even revealed commandments must be understood before they can be obeyed. If a commentary may be permitted to apply Pauline teaching to its contemporary situation, then this commentary wishes to accuse the non-intellectual, non-doctrinal so-called Christianity of this century of being seriously heretical. There is no excuse for disparaging the truth of the Biblical propositions.

What is less clear in the verse is the meaning of "if you think otherwise, even this God will reveal to you." One of the interpretations is that God will reveal the truth to those who think that Paul does not pursue the heavenly calling. But were there any in Philippi who thought so meanly of Paul? The somewhat disreputable preachers of 1:15 do not seem to have questioned Paul's zeal. They were simply jealous.

Another interpretation is that the "otherwise" refers to Paul's views on sanctification. Perhaps they thought that God did not require so much zeal. This is a plausible interpretation, for it is very likely, almost always, that some church members, if not in word, at least in deed, or the lack of deeds, do rather less than they should.

In this connection one should note the *ti* in *ti eterōs:* otherwise about anything. This removes all restrictions on the limits of disagreement. Of course sanctification itself presents a broad front. It includes innumerable thoughts and actions. But *anything* is still wider. Is this what Paul meant? Eadie tends toward this view, and its extent allows him to say, "the difference of view was not some wilful and wicked misconception . . . adhered to with inveterate or malignant obstinacy. It was rather some truth not fully seen in all its bearings . . ." (207).

This interpretation receives some support from the initial conjunction of the phrase. Instead of translating it "and if," one could say, "even if," with the suggestion that it is not very likely. One must note that Paul is speaking, not to all Christians, but to the mature, among whom there would be greater unanimity of mind. But even so, does it seem likely that God will shortly reveal to us the solution to all the difficulties we meet in Scripture? The differences among commentators do not seem to bear this out. The verse itself is an instance: What did Paul mean by "even this God will reveal"?

A more important point comes in this reference to revelation. Bible-believing Christians all agree that God gave verbal revelations to the apostles. Did God also give such to the Philippians, the Ephesians, and to us today? Some Pentecostalists think so. Others sort of give the same impression without stating it so distinctly. There was a college professor–and of course college professors always think clearly–who was considering resigning his position. There seemed to be a better opening elsewhere. So, he and his wife took it to the Lord in prayer. Moreover, as he told me plainly, they "put out the fleece." If the other position offered him a higher salary, he would take it. Gideon, you will remember, put out the fleece twice. My friend needed only one test. In conformity with the apostolic prerogatives and privileges as indicated here and there in both Testaments, one must conclude that Paul promised the Philippians the illumination of the Spirit, not an additional verbal revelation. The Philippians had understood much of what Paul preached. They failed to understand other parts of his preaching, and, as we all do, failed to trace out the implications very far. But if we meditate on the revealed words day and night, some of those implications will dawn on us in the light of the Spirit.

Verse 17 forms a sort of intermediate conclusion. Paul does what few of us would dare to do: set himself up as an example. He had done so before. 1 Corinthians 4:16 says, "Be ye followers of me." 1 Corinthians 11:1 says, "Be ye followers of me even as I also am of Christ." Well, most of us follow afar off. So far off that we cannot accuse Paul of pride.

3:18, 19   For many walk, whom I often mentioned to

Chapter Three

> you, and now even weeping mention, enemies of the cross of Christ, whose end destruction, whose god is their belly, and whose glory is in their shame, who think on earthly [matters].

It would be a mistake to see in these verses a reference to those whom Paul gently corrected in verse 15. The only connection is that those obvious enemies of Christ give us stronger reasons for pursuing a godly life. Hendriksen believes that these enemies were professing Christians. The description makes this hardly plausible. Yet Ellicott also identifies them as "nominal Christians, baptized sinners ... of an Epicurian bias" (94).

Incidentally, the Epicureans do not deserve the poor reputation that has been given to them. Epicurus did not make his belly his god: He was satisfied with plain fare; and instead of being or recommending licentiousness, he encouraged celibacy.

Lenski seems to think that Paul has the Judaizers in mind. They were indeed enemies of the cross, but their food laws certainly prevented them from making their belly their god. Nor did they, at least in a common usage of the words, confine their thinking to earthly things. However mistaken the Judaizers may have been, they believed they were serving Jehovah, and not the world. Furthermore, had Paul meant the Judaizers, he would probably have been incensed against them, as in Galatians, rather than weeping because of them. Furthermore again, though in reality the Judaizers made the cross of Christ of none effect, they did not think they were opposing the cross. When one characterizes a group, one usually mentions some point that both they themselves and their opponents acknowledge.

Müller defends their identification as Judaizers on the ground that Paul does not call these people simply enemies of the cross, but definitely says they are *the* enemies of the cross. Certainly one cannot logically make this inference from the presence of the article. The reference to their belly is a much clearer indication

102   *Philippians*

that the Judaizers are not these enemies.

Though it is not conclusive, the phrase "whose glory is in their shame" seems to indicate licentiousness. If this be so, then the reference must be to some Gentiles, for the Judaizers never had the reputation of being licentious. Martin attempts (158) to identify this shame with "the nakedness of the human body which was required for the rite [of circumcision] to be performed." But if this were so the circumcision of all infants, including those who later became prophets–Moses, Elijah, Zechariah–was shameful. And if shameful, circumcision must have been an ungodly ceremony.

This method of elimination leaves only Gentile heathen–perhaps a few church members–who took an active part in tempting, seducing, ridiculing, opposing the Christian believers. Note that Paul says "many." Though not conclusive, *many* fits the heathen better than it fits the Jews or Judaizers.

3:20, 21   **For our citizenship pertains to Heaven, from which also we await the Savior and Lord Jesus Christ, who will change the form of the body of our humiliation [so as to be] conformed to the body of his glory according to the energy of his being able even to subject the universe to himself.**

One or two grammatical notes: the first (second in Greek) word, *for,* regularly designates a reason for what precedes, but sometimes the reason is stated negatively or by opposition, as here. The last word, *himself* (third from last in Greek) has been left unaspirated in most modern texts–for example, Nestle, and Tischendorf. The Aland group is to be commended for using a rough breathing, as the sense very obviously requires.

The word *our,* in "our citizenship," is emphatic by position. It strengthens the contrast with those whose thinking is occupied with earthly interests. The word translated *citizenship* is an hapaxlegomenon. It can mean the State, the constitution, or the functions of a citizen. Hendriksen uses "homeland."

Some sects draw peculiar conclusions. There are differences among various groups of Amish and Mennonites. Some withdraw more than others from civil affairs. One remembers with admiration how the Amish in Lancaster County refused government relief during the depression of the thirties. The church takes care of its own. Most, if not all, refuse to vote. Many will serve in the armed forces as medics, but not as combatants. Their heroism is unquestioned. Usually their children do not attend public schools. Some seem to accept no responsibility for punishing crime or curtailing drug addiction and abortion. One group at least is so non-resistant that they will not defend themselves from an attacker. They reduce their contacts with society to the inescapable minimum—because their citizenship is in Heaven. Here they are strangers and aliens. While one must admire their sincerity and consistency, their interpretation of Scripture is questionable. Although Christ said, "My kingdom is not of this world, else would my servants fight"—and this referred precisely to rescuing him from execution—Christ also said, "I have also sent them into the world," and "I pray not that thou shouldst take them out of the world." To this the Amish can of course reply that indeed they are in the world and that they are not going to commit suicide. But being in the world they must render certain things to Caesar, they must honor the king, pay taxes, and bear arms. They must resist evil and try to prevent crime. Dare the Amish man say that it is wrong for him to use force against a marauder who has broken into his house and is attempting to rape his wife? Such non-resistance is surely not Christian conduct. Nor can he on Biblical grounds deny his social or civil responsibilities.

Unfortunately, for most Christians it is our heavenly citizenship, not our earthly citizenship, which needs emphasis. If *politeuma* is translated *country* or *native land,* as is possible, a question arises as to the words "from which." Since the *which* is singular, strict grammar would have it refer to our *country,* which word therefore should not be translated *citizenship*. Such is the view of Moule and Lenski. Eadie and some others make the *which* refer to Heaven, even though *Heaven* in Greek is plural. Since Christ is usually portrayed as returning from Heaven, Eadie has a point. Grammar is sometimes flexible. It doesn't make much difference, anyhow.

"From which we also await the Savior" It may come as a shock to many who do not read the Bible carefully that the term *savior* is not very often applied to Christ: In fact less than half a dozen times; and it is also rare in early Christian literature. The Gnostics used it rather frequently; but its most common use was as a title of the Roman Emperor. Today evangelicals use it profusely. Well, it does have some Scriptural support.

More interesting and more important than the usage of a title is the statement of what Christ will do when he returns: He will change the form of our bodies. There is some question as to whether *body* in this sentence designates only and strictly our physical body or whether it is meant to include our soul too. Either way, it is the physical body that causes the more perplexity.

The catechism says, "their bodies, still being united to Christ, do rest in their graves until the resurrection." But many bodies have no grave. The Reformers whom Bloody Mary burned alive had no graves. The early Christians whom Nero fed to the lions had no graves. Even poor Yorick, who was buried, had no body when the gravediggers could find only a skull. How then can our bodies be raised from the dead? Christ's body was most exceptional, for he had been buried on Friday afternoon and was raised Sunday morning. Scirpture also says that "he saw no corruption." Lazarus had.

The resurrection and the transformation of our bodies are in the realm of the miraculous and do not lend themselves to much explanation. To reduce the difficulties only one or two things can be said. First, Christ's resurrection body was quite different from his previous body. The account seems to say that he could pass through a closed door, and presumably could travel distances instantaneously. His new body was not always recognizable, for the woman at the tomb and the two on the road to Emmaus did not identify him. Later his body ascended into the clouds, as we cannot; and possibly his body changed still further. Then, second, and more prosaically, we ourselves, now in this life, do not have the same physical body all our years. A popular notion has it that we get a completely new body every seven years. The time is probably incorrect, but it is clear that the visible components of our bodies enter and leave at various intervals. Plato gives an interesting illustration: The soul is like a weaver who weaves various coats, so that when one wears out another is ready. Hume has a less imaginative example: A ship may be repaired after each voyage, until not one of the original parts remain; but we call it the same ship because the change has been gradual, continuous, and the purpose remains the same. Plato's illustration better fits the idea of immortality. But none of this helps very much, for the final resurrection is not only strange to our ordinary experience, it is also quite different from the cases recounted in Scripture. Not only will there be the marvellous changes hinted at in 1 Corinthians 15, but included specifically in 1 Corinthians 6:13 is the destruction of the stomach and its food.

No wonder Paul says that Christ will re-form our humble bodies by the power of his being able to subject the entire universe to himself. It takes that much power to do so, and Christ has that much power.

CHAPTER FOUR

4:1   Consequently, my beloved and longed for brethren, my joy and crown, so stand in the Lord, beloved.

It would have been more logical for the original editor to begin chapter four with the next verse. Whoever it was who inserted the chapters and verses was deficient in logic. The exhortation of this verse clearly, even without the explicit *ōste,* is the concluding line of what precedes and has nothing to do with what follows.

Although the verb *epipotheō* occurs nine times in the New Testament, this adjective, "longed-for," is a hapaxlegomenon. The fact is worth noting because liberal critics occasionally try to argue against the Pauline authorship of this or that epistle on the basis of its containing one or two hapaxlegomena. Nonsense. Many authors use a word only once. I suspect that this commentary has at least one, but such is no indication of authorship.

Though some commentators go into raptures over Paul's tremendous emotion in calling the Philippians his joy and crown, the emotion may seem somewhat misplaced to us. It is true that the Philippians had sent financial aid to Paul, and it is true that his personal relationship to them was one of great affection. But could it have been so much more than his affection for the Ephesians or Corinthians? Eadie suggests that the phrase "joy and crown" was "a common one," and however sincere was not so ecstatic as a modern reader might suppose it to be. Natually Paul had tender memories of the Christians at Philippi, and they did not present him with the many troubles he faced in the Corinthian church. But he did have one.

4:2,3 I beseech Euodia and I beseech Syntyche that they think the same thing in the Lord. Yes, I request even you, G.S., to bring them together, these women who contended with me in [extending] the Gospel with also Clement and my other co-workers, whose names [are] in the book of life.

Two women had a falling out over some difference of opinion. It could not have been a matter of theology, for if it were, Paul would have clearly decided it. He came down hard on false teachers. This matter was so inconsequential that he does not mention it. He just wants them to kiss and make up. Evidently the disagreement was sharp enough to trouble or hamper the congregation to some extent and Paul therefore asks G.S. to help. In Germany many family names are trade names: Schmidt, Müller, Bauer, Schleiermacher, and Schwarzerde, whom we know in Greek as Melanchthon. Here the Greek word *Gnēsie* is not a first name: It means *genuine, sincere,* or *true. Suzuge* (vocative case) means *yoke-fellow.* Even the Revised Standard Version so translates it. So does the New International Version. But some commentators take it as a family name, Mr. Sugugos. There is one good reason for thinking so. Unless it is a proper name, and if there were as many as two men in the Philippian church, the church members, to all of whom the letter was addressed, would not know which man was meant. Some commentators suggest a play on words, as if in 1825 one might have said, you ought to get your wife a better veil, Herr Schleiermacher. Then too, the mention of Clement would be strange if Paul had not named his main peacemaker. A slighter reason for taking *Suzugos* as a proper name is the fact that Paul regularly calls his co-workers *sunergoi,* not *suzugoi.* Those who do not take it as a proper name sometimes indulge in unrestrained guesswork. One even suggests Lydia, in spite of the fact that the adjective is masculine. Christ himself and Paul's brother are on the list. Also Timothy, in spite of the fact that he is a sort of co-writer of the letter. And there are other guesses, mere guesses. Why not guess that Suzugos is a proper name? Some also guess that the Clement mentioned here is the man we know as Clement of Rome. The epistle shows him only as Clement of Philippi, and no doubt every city had several Clements.

The two women in view were not the only ones who greatly helped Paul in Philippi, nor was Clement the third and last. There were "the others." Their names are not given in this book, but they are inexpungeably (a hapaxlegomenon) inscribed in the Lamb's Book of Life. He who began the good work will complete it.

4:4 **Rejoice in the Lord always; again I will say rejoice. Let your gentleness be known to all men. The Lord is near.**

This verse begins a new paragraph without special reference to the preceding verse. It can be regarded as the beginning of a somewhat long-drawn-out concluding section. The force of its initial command bears in on us when we remember that Paul was in jail; and still more when we remember that Paul had been in jail at Philippi. There at midnight Paul and Silas had sung praises to God. Perhaps, I say only perhaps, we could also sing praises in a Philippian jail or in a Roman dungeon. But can we rejoice when the denomination to which we have for years been attached declines into apostasy? Can we rejoice at the murder of Protestants in Northern Ireland? Can we rejoice when a million American mothers murder a million babies? Can a man rejoice when he fails to celebrate his golden wedding anniversary by one year? Yet Paul's wife had died too.*

Paul next urges gentleness or forbearance. Pastors, and pas-

---

* If Paul had been a member of the Sanhedrin, as Acts may imply, he would have been a married man.

tors' wives, need a large share of forbearance, in view of senseless dissensions within a congregation. Euodia and Syntyche are still a pain in the neck. In this day of extreme feminism, I can add that the most senseless disturber of the peace in thirty years of one congregation's history was a man. And I well remember a young elder, completely blameless, who humbly apologized for an imaginary slight.

However much forbearance is necessary for congregational harmony, and however much it may in the long run impress "all men," Paul's epistle to the Galatians describes a situation where forbearance would undermine the Gospel. If twentieth century Christians are somewhat lacking in forbearance, they are much more lacking in New Testament denunciation of false teachers. Even in Philippians Paul gives such instruction at the beginning of chapter three. But it seems not to have been needed in Philippi as much as in other places. It is one of the greatest needs at this end of the twentieth century.

There may be many, though related, reasons for forbearance and gentleness. The one Paul gives may be taken as inclusive of all: "The Lord is at hand."

Ellicott seems convinced that this phrase refers to Christ's second coming. One might argue: I need not insist on my rights, I can accept insults and injuries, because the Lord will soon return to avenge me and punish our enemies. Or less legalistically, I can support such trials because I shall soon enjoy eternal bliss. Hendriksen as well as Ellicott accepts this interpretation. Martin says, "the eschatological sense of the Lord's coming to vindicate his oppressed people requires" this interpretation. Yet in spite of the near unanimity of this view, it strikes me that the general context of the epistle has much less to do with persecution than with daily annoyances, either within the congregation, or else also in the civil community. Though persecution had begun, it rather clearly had not attained its later virulence. Remember that Paul had not been imprisoned in Philippi for preaching theology, but, as in Ephesus, for economic disturbances. Hence, in disagreement

110 Philippians

with the large majority, I think Paul is telling them that when annoyances come, they should remember Christ's omnipresence. This quieter and less turbulent view seems to be supported in the next verse and one or two later verses.

4:6 **Be troubled by nothing, but in everything, by prayer and petition, with thanksgiving, let your requests be made known to God.**

The support this verse gives to the interpretation of the previous verse could have been a bit more emphasized by repeating the usual translation. Do not be *anxious* about anything. But the words *nothing* and *everything* are emphatic enough. Indeed, the word *nothing* is emphatic by position. One also remembers that Christ used these same two words, *mēden merimnate,* in Matthew 6:25. These words are more inclusive than congregational annoyances, but neither are they restricted to savage persecution. The main group seems to be daily disappointments and troublesome trials.

The verse also teaches something about prayer. Prayers usually, if not absolutely always, should contain thanksgiving. We may properly pray about anything at all: In everything let your requests ascend to the throne of grace. In view of the word *everything,* one should note that not all prayers should be restricted to generalities. The pastoral prayers in the worship service should for the most part be general. The minister is not offering his own prayer, he is leading the congregation in prayer. Therefore his terminology should be appropriate for each one. Usually, though there may be unusual exceptions, everybody should make the prayer his own; and if someone cannot, either this one has some hidden sin he does not want to confess, or the minister does not properly understand his ministerial responsibilities. Both types of flaw are possible. But when it comes to individual prayer, the situation is different. A certain Directory for Worshp, whose exact provenance I most unfortunately cannot at the moment remember, stresses the fact that although individual prayers very properly include generalities, one must also confess sins in particular and may include particular requests. It is not enough to say, "Forgive me, Lord, for I constantly sin in thought, word, and deed." We must say, "Forgive me, Lord, for I lied to Mr. Smith this morning."

4:7 And the peace of God, which surpasses every mind, will guard your hearts and your thoughts by Christ Jesus.

Motyer writes that this verse is a "promise that our lives will be touched with the evidence of the supernatural" (167). Below he adds, "what the church and the individual believer needs more than anything today . . . is the touch of the supernatural." Such flowery language is too easily misunderstood. In fact there is nothing in it to understand. We do not live charmed lives, we neither receive new verbal revelations nor experience miracles. Yet, as we shall happily note in a moment, Motyer is not so bad as his fuzzy phrase suggested. He is one of the few who see the real meaning of the verse.

Eadie does not see it, or hardly sees it. He wrote, the peace of this verse is "but another name for happiness" (253). Moule identifies the peace of God with "inward serenity" (81). Hendriksen agrees: "If joy in the Lord reigns *within* [ital. his] the heart . . . the result will be peace"; and "It is the heart's calm after Calvary's storm" (196). Martin explicitly distinguishes between the two meanings of peace and explicitly accepts inward serenity. He speaks of "careworn and fretful hearts" and their "enjoyment of God's peace which he has promised to all who are harassed . . ." (170). And on the next page he speaks of "inner tranquility." Such is a very common view.

But surely this is a mistaken view. Some Christians are serene. Paul himself was not always so. In the second place, it does not seem to me that mere subjective serenity can guard us against anything. There must be a better interpretation. Eadie himself acknowledges that Augustine and Anselm viewed it as objective peace. The peace of God is the opposite of the enmity of God. We were once God's enemies, but God made peace by the blood of his Son. One of Augustine's phrases was, "the peace wherewith God himself is pacified" (*De Civitas Dei,* XXII, 29). And to do justice to Motyer, we quote, "the 'God of peace' is the God who makes peace between himself and sinners" (168).

If serenity is a poor guard against disaster, can the peace of God be a good guard? Yes, regeneration and its consequent faith guards us against everlasting destruction from the presence of the Lord. And this has been accomplished "by Christ Jesus."

With this interpretation of the peace of God the reader can much better understand what Paul means when he says that it surpasses every mind. Serenity may sometimes be unusual, but it hardly surpasses all human understanding. If this be granted, the next step is to examine the phrase "surpassing every mind." One of the poorer interpretations in my opinion is that expressed by Jacobus Müller: "the peace which God gives excels and surpasses all our own intellectual calculations . . . and premeditated ideas of how to get rid of our cares" (142). The first objection to this is the previous one that he makes the peace of God subjective serenity. The second, in conformity with the first, pictures God as more clever than the man who cannot figure a way out of his predicaments. God is smarter than I am, much as Einstein also was. Martin puts the disjunction clearly: "The descriptive phrase . . . may signify 'achieving more than our clever forethought and ingenious plans can accomplish'; or, 'transcending every human thought' . . . beyond the range of our comprehension" (170). Though he fails to see how outwardly it fits his inner serenity, Martin's acceptance of the second alternative is absolutely correct. The most cursory consideration of human history, from Sennacherib to Chairman Mao, as resulting in surpassing good because controlled by a God who sees the end from the beginning and does all things well, supports this second interpretation. History is beyond our comprehension.

On the other hand, it is wise to warn against exaggerated views of God's incomprehensibility. If we imprison God in darkness unapproachable and full of paradox, we discard the whole Bible as unintelligible. God has revealed to us many of his truths which we can understand, some easily, some with difficulty. No one needs to know all about the Trinity, no one needs to know half of what the Bible teaches about the Trinity, to understand clearly that David was King of Israel, or that Abraham worshipped Jehovah. This point, which most commentators in the past never discussed, is especially important today in this age of unmitigated irrationalism. God never revealed anything that the human mind cannot understand, for all Scripture, all of it, is profitable for doctrine.

4:8, 9   As for the rest, brethren, whatever things are true, whatever noble, whatever just, whatever holy, whatever lovely, whatever of good fame, if any virtue, if any praise, think on those things. What things also you learned, and received and heard and saw in me, these things, do. And the God of peace will be with you.

These two verses are commonly explained as an exhortation to morality. And so they are. But, not so one-sidedly as the exponents of non-doctrinal Christianity suppose. For non-doctrinal Christianity is not Christianity. As Lenski says, "Some eliminate doctrine and restrict the list to conduct. True, these things refer to conduct, yet not so as though conduct could ever be divorced from doctrine" (881). Note that the main verb is *think*. Note also that the first specification is *truth*.

The word *conduct* is itself misleading and ambiguous. The common idea is that conduct is overt, bodily behavior. Thinking is not "conduct." This is similar to the emphasis some professing Christians put on *experience*. For them experience is metaphorical palpitation of the heart, but not the memorization of Greek irregular verbs so as to be able to read the New Testament. Meditating on the Trinity or on the federal headship of Adam is both experience and conduct. Hence when Martin says, "The Bible is not concerned with mental reflection for its own sake, but only as it promotes behavior" (171), his statement is seriously ambiguous and almost always misleading. It ignores all those verses in Scripture whose aim, whose immediate aim at least, is to teach us the truth. Indeed without the intellectual cerebration which these myopic pragmatists despise, one can see no connection between the intertrinitarian relationship and honesty in business. I could specify two congregations, one more fundamentalistic, the other more anthropocentric, where malicious gossip is heard more frequently than theological sermons.

The list of virtues, of which truth is the first, is rather general in expression. We are to think on things that are noble and lovely, but the specific things are not listed. How can Lenski say, "Paul defines 'these things' in a new way, in one that is concrete and personal" (884)? Obviously this is not so. It would be hard to find words more general and less specific. Paul mentions truth, but not the details of David's kingship. Well, naturally. The six *whatevers* and the two *anythings* are completely generic. One interesting and unimportant point is that *virtue,* seventh in the list, is very infrequently–only three times–mentioned in the New Testament; whereas it appears quite regularly in pagan ethical literature. One commentator suggests that that is the reason the New Testament writers avoid the word. I doubt it. The Greek word generally means excellence, and often physical prowess, so that here we must not suppose it restricted to its common English and American connotation, which when attributed to women means chastity. Eadie tells us that older Scottish usage makes it mean thrift and industry.

The Nestlé text notes some manuscripts that add *epistēmē* after *epainos, knowledge* after *praise.* The reading is spurious, though it shows that some Christians in the sixth and ninth centuries thought that Paul was again stressing knowledge.

In verse nine Paul points to himself as both a teacher and example of these Christian qualities.

At this point the conclusion and the epistle might have ended; but it seems that Paul suddenly thought of something else that needed to be added. Hence come verses 10-20, after which he sends his final greetings.

4:10 **I greatly rejoiced in the Lord that just now your thought of me has blossomed in that you were always thinking about me, but had no opportunity.**

This is a very difficult verse to translate literally, as Eadie also admits (265). No English, however crabbed, seems to offer the necessary accuracy with the desired imitation of the Greek construction. The polished versions are quite satisfactory. With the help of verse 18 it seems that Paul had received a gift from the Philippians, a gift delayed by what circumstances we do not know. The embarrassed language of this paragraph is the result of Paul's principle to support himself as much as possible and not be a financial burden to the churches. One may surmise that he could not manufacture many tents in prison. If a minister has to moonlight, the extension of the Gospel suffers. When a man has spent four years in college, and three in seminary, and has spent a goodly sum doing so, his training makes him too valuable a person to waste time supporting himself and a family. Nor ought he to be deprived of a wife and family. Nor ought the wife find it necessary to earn needed support. A regular and sufficient salary should remove obsequious embarrassment.

A slight grammatical point exercises some of the commentators. The first verb is aorist: *rejoiced.* The Revised Standard Version and the New International Version take it as an "epistolary" aorist and translate it as a present tense. Lenski points out, as anyone might, that it is simple statement of fact. A hurried reader may fail to note that Paul does not thank them for their gift. When one comes to realize this, one naturally asks, why? Apparently the gift had come some time back; Eadie thinks as much as five years. Paul, accordingly, had thanked them earlier. It seems to have been a substantial gift. The lack of opportunity may have been that no one was traveling from Philippi to Rome for some time. Then too, although the churches in Macedonia were very generous (2 Corinthians 8:1-2), their "trial of affliction," stagnation, inflation, depression, or whatever, may have hindered their raising much money for several years. But these possibilities are mostly guesswork. At any rate the verb *rejoiced* is aorist.

4:11 **Not that I speak because of lack, for I myself learned to be self-sufficient in what [circumstances] I am.**

The word *lack* is our word *hysteria;* but the English term has become too strong and too specific. *Lack* is a quite correct translation. The apostle was never hysterical.

He *learned* is aorist again. We might have expected a perfect, but Paul learned his lesson so well and so far in the past that he uses a simple aorist.

Self-sufficient is a good Stoic term. Even today we speak of a man's being *stoical,* when he is unaffected by reverses and tragedies. The Stoics stressed virtue, not pleasure; external conditions were insignificant, the important thing was our reaction to them. This is not to say that their morality or religion was Christian. Their approval of suicide was unchristian and their social conservatism supported official polytheism, though actually they were mono- or pan-theistic. The later Roman Stoics, however, as distinguished from those of 300 B.C., would speak of God as Father. Their *Logos*-doctrine, through pantheistic, derived from Heraclitus, helped the Christians, or at least stimulated the Christians to study John 1:1 and eventually, through Tertullian, arrive at the Athanasian doctrine of the Trinity. This is not at all to say that the contents of the Nicene Creed came from the Stoics, much less from Plato who had no *Logos* doctrine. Tertullian himself was ardently opposed to Greek philosophy. But he was stimulated by it nonetheless, and more so than Athanasius was. Well, this discursion has left self-sufficiency far behind, and the further exposition can best return to the next verse.

4:12 **I know both how to be humbled, I know also how to abound; in everything and in all things I have learned both to eat well and to starve, both to abound and to be in want.**

Starve may be too strong a word; *be hungry* might be better. In any case these three oppositions give the specifications for the preceding verse. The whole has to do with physical conditions, conditions that vary with one's finances. The first pair of contraries might in a different context refer to spiritual affairs, but the latter two contraries, and the whole context, determine the correct sense.

Incidentally, anyone who has found this commentary too detailed and too much adumbrated with–that means, put under the shadow of–grammatical trivialities, should try to read Ellicott. But such a one would have put aside this commentary before getting to 4:12, and hence would be saved the unpleasantness of reading perhaps the first ten verses in Ellicott.

As for these two verses there is little grammatical to say, and not much exegetically either. Eadie rambles on for five and a half pages, quoting Jeremy Taylor "with his wonted wealth of genius," referring to Pelagius and Calvin, and explaining it all no more clearly than Paul's own adequate words. Müller says all that needs to be said–in two short paragraphs.

There is one question, however, that some readers, if they know something about the Greek mystery religions, might like to ask about the verb *memuēmai*. Above it was translated simply as "I have learned." This verb became a technical term for initiation into the mysteries, a fact which led some liberals to use it in their support of the theory that Paul's theology was dependent on these pagan cults. This is poor thinking, for there are English words which, though now used as technical terms, such as *force* and *mass,* still retain their original popular meanings also.

4:13, 14 **I can do all things by him who strengthens me. Except you did well, sharing with me in my distress.**

The Textus Receptus and King James have "by Christ who strengthens me." Of course this makes good sense; but the manuscript evidence is poor, and the article, here translated *him who,* makes it awkward. Once again, for it is a pet point of mine, the preposition *en* means *by,* not *in.*

Verse 14 assures the Philippians that his dependence on Christ does not prevent him from appreciating their gift.

4:15, 16 **You also know, Philippians, that in the beginning of the Gospel, when I went out from Macedonia, no church shared with me in an account of giving and receiving, except you only; because even in Thessalonica, both once and twice, you sent to me for my need.**

The word *account* and the phrase "giving and receiving" are business or commercial terms. They are used as we speak of a bank account or charge account. Another minor matter: If a few verses here and there from other parts of the New Testament help to explain a verse in Philippians, the verse here sheds some light on John 1:1. These two verses contain the term *logos.* In Philippians it is clear that the word does not mean *word.* Nor can it in John mean *account. Logos* has many meanings, at least a dozen or more. Only infrequently does it mean *word.* Therefore John 1:1 is poorly translated. The mistake, so far as I know, goes back to Jerome, who used the Latin term *verbum*. Reason, Logic, Law, are better than sentence, ratio, pretext, and argument. As a philosophic term Heraclitus and the Stoics used it to designate the supreme law of the universe, an intelligence who steers Heaven and Earth. The Jewish philosopher, Philo of Alexandria, greatly influenced by Stoicism, used the term to designate the mind of God, and he used it with so much literary embellishment that later Christians thought he had almost arrived at the New Testament doctrine of the Trinity. This is a misunderstanding of Philo. But John 1:1 says that Christ was the Reason, the Logic, the Intelligence, the Mind of God. Athanasius later argued that Christ was the only word God ever spoke.

If remarks on John seem irrelevant to an explanation of Philippians, one might forgive their insertion on the ground that these verses in Philippians hardly need any explanation.

4:17, 18   **Not that I seek the gift; rather I seek the fruit which increases your account *(logon)*. I receive everything in full and abound. I am full, having received from Epaphroditus what came from you, an odor of sweet smell, an acceptable sacrifice, well pleasing to God.**

These verses also need little explanation. The commercial language was noted in the previous comments, and the Old Testament language of offering and sacrifice is unmistakable. What may merit a remark is the apparent embarrassment Paul shows in these ten or so verses. He seems to overdo his appreciation. A plausible explanation is that the Philippians, in a period of financial depression, had sent him a surprisingly munificent gift. It is as if the widow who threw in tuppence had thrown in a hundred shekels.

4:19   **But my God will fill your every need according to his wealth in glory by Christ Jesus.**

Note that here is another instance in which *en* means *by*. I have found that this seemingly grammatical triviality clarifies numbers of verses.

In view of the fact that the idea of financial aid has dominated this section of the chapter, one wonders whether the "every need" which God supplies is more material than spiritual. Is Paul saying, your recession will soon be over? This does not tie in too well with the Old Testament references to a sweet odor of incense on the altar. Furthermore, "in glory by Christ Jesus" does not have a commercial tone.

If, however, we stress spiritual blessings, can we say that God supplies *every* need? We no doubt need advancement in sanctification and wisdom; but do we not also need food and clothing, if not a Mercedes Benz? Chrysostom seems to limit the needs to these material blessings. Surely Paul meant both. Meyer seems to include both temporal and heavenly blessings; but then he peculiarly limits the giving of these gifts either to the millennium or to Heaven also. Meyer often seems too preoccupied with the millennium. It repeatedly distorts his exegesis. One commentator replied to him: "If the apostle says of himself *peplērōmai,* who should he in *plērōsei* refer to the day of the second coming for the supply of every want?" The phrase "in glory" does not necessitate such a future reference. We could translate it: God will gloriously satisfy your every need.

The difficulty today's Christian has with this verse lies in the fact that if God supplies our every need, he does not satisfy our every want. He will not do so for Paul. Read the disturbing account of Paul's life in 2 Corinthians 11:23-28. Can we, with lesser troubles say

4:20   To God and our Father, glory to the age of ages, Amen.

Most of the commentators slurp on this verse as if it were a bowl of soup. Lenski is more circumspect. When there is nothing to be explained, it is foolish to explain it. This verse is the logical end of the epistle. Paul adds only a greeting or salutation.

4:21, 22, 23 Greet every saint in Christ Jesus. The brethren who are with me greet you. All the saints greet you, especially those of Caesar's household. The grace of the Lord Jesus Christ [be] with your spirit, Amen.

As with the preceding verses there is little to explain here. Yet a few points should be mentioned. First, because of lesser significance, the textual critics, in opposition to overwhelming manuscript evidence, delete the final *Amen*. Of rather more importance is the mention of Caesar's "household." One can hardly believe that it means the emperor's immediate family. It could possibly designate some of the palace guard, or various servants, of whom there were probably a large number. But at any rate the Gospel had penetrated the emperor's entourage. The commentators sometimes suggest that many of these had been converted earlier, even before they had been brought to Rome. But clearly Paul had converted some of them. As often in a Christian community there are subdivisions. This does not mean that there was any ill-will. Nevertheless, the Jewish Christians would show mutual affection. There were some, maybe both Jews and Gentiles, who were closer to Paul, whom Paul now designates as "those who are with me"; and thus there are "all the saints." These divisions show that Christianity had made gratifying progress in Rome.

The grace of the Lord Jesus Christ be with your spirit, Amen.

Concluding Remarks

The aim of this commentary, as of the writer's previous attempts, has been to clarify the meaning of the epistle. If properly done, it should be of interest of all Christians–should be because the Bible tells us to meditate on its message day and night. What Christian can dare ignore, wittingly, a revelation from God; but multitudes do so unwittingly. The cares of this world choke and stifle a faint desire to study the Bible. Many church members hardly even read it.

A greater responsibility rests on the ministers of the Gospel. These men are supposed to *minister,* to *serve,* to dispense the Gospel to their congregations. Many do not do so, at least to any great extent. They may serve a quick lunch, but never a six course dinner. I have heard preachers berate "dead orthodoxy," and in varying terminology tell the people that it doesn't make much difference what one believes, so long as he lives right. These ministers, so many of whom I myself have heard, are not liberals, modernists, or neo-orthodox: They may even believe that the Bible is inerrant, but they are not interested in understanding much of its content. They condemn other ministers and members who know too much theology and who live evil lives. Well, I have met many who say this, but I don't remember meeting any of those they so describe. My sneaking suspicion is that they are too lazy to study, or too incompetent. Some of them may condemn dead orthodoxy as a disguise to hide their own unacknowledged unbelief. But in any case, witting or unwitting, stupid or sly, lazy or otherwise preoccupied, these ministers disparage the Bible. For the Bible urges meditation, thought, study, reflection, reasoning, contemplation, inquiry, research, scrutiny, analysis–well, that is a fair enough sample from Roget's *Thesaurus.*

From the Bible, the Bible they avoid studying too much, one may quote, the entrance of the dry as dust theology giveth light–well, at least I didn't put quotation marks on it. But theology is dry as dust only for those whose mind is a desert. Now, as for quotation marks, try these:

"Sanctify them through thy truth, thy word is truth." Can one make progress in real sanctification without understanding the word?

"If a man keep my word, he shall not see death, ever."

"All things that pertain to life and godliness come throught the knowledge of him that called us."

"Wisdom and knowledge shall be the stability of thy times," or "A wealth of salvation, wisdom, and knowledge."

"The fear of the Lord is the beginning of knowledge, but fools despise wisdom and instruction."

And finally, "All Scripture is profitable for doctrine . . . that the man of God may be thoroughly furnished unto all good works."

INDEX

abortion/abortionists, 82, 103
Abraham, 113
Absalom, 75
accuracy, 115
achri, 9
Adam, 99, 114
addiction, 103
agape, 49
agony, 44
aid, financial, 7
aisthēsis, 21
Aland, Kurt, 24, 52, 87, 102
Albuquerque, 3
ambiguity, 45
American Revised Version, viii, 15, 68
American Standard Version, 6, 34, 80
Amish, 103
angel, 59, 68
Anglicans, 3
Anselm, 112
apologetics, 28
apologia, 18, 28
Apology of Socrates, The (Plato), 18, 91
apostasy, 108
apostle(s), 2, 37, 44, 71, 81, 100
aproskopoi, 22
Aquinas, Thomas, 4
argumentation, 28
Arians, 67
Aristarchus, 79
Aristotle, 46, 50; *Works:*
Constitution of Athens, 90; *Physics*, ix
Arius, 67
Arminianism, 2, 10-14, 16, 70-71, 73-74, 91, 96
Arminius, 71
Arndt, W. F., 47, 72, 91, 98
ascension, 67
assurance, 14, 16-17, 29, 31, 74
Athanasius, 117
atheism, 33, 76
atonement, 85, 91
Augsburg Confession, 59
Augustine, 20, 55, 112; *Works: De Civitas Dei*, 112; *De Trinitate*, 55
Authorized Version, *see* King James Version
authorship, Pauline, 106
awe, 74

barbarism, 45
Barnabas, 28, 51, 85
Barth, Karl, 40
bebaiōsei, 18
bebaiōsis, 18
being, 55-56
Belgic Confession, 59
belief, 39
benediction, 4
Benjamin, 88
Bible, x, 3, 19, 59, 74, 104, 113-114, 122; *see also* Scripture

Biblical Predestination (Clark), 72
bishops, 1, 4
Bithynia, 37
Black, Matthew, 87
Blass, F., 8, 50, 92
body, 105
Bruce, A. B., 65; *Works: The Humiliation of Christ*, 65
business, 114
Buswell, Jr., J. Oliver, 94

Caesar, 25, 103, 121
call, effectual, 10, 16
Calvin, John, 62, 74, 117
Calvinism, 10, 12-13, 40, 71, 91
Cambridge Bible Commentary on the New English Bible (Grayston), ix
catechism, 104
causality, 91
celibacy, 101
Christianity, 29, 41
Chrysostom, 6, 36, 55-56, 120
church, 3-4, 16, 37, 51-52, 69, 88, 111, 122
circumcision, 88, 102
citizenship, 38, 102
De Civitas Dei (Augustine), 112
Clark, Gordon H., 12, 72; *Works: Biblical Predestination*, 72; "Determinism and Responsibility," 75; *Predestination*, 72; *Predestination in the Old Testament*, 72; *What Do Presbyterians Believe?* 12
Clement of Rome, 36, 108
Colosse, vii

commandments, 31, 99
communicatio idiomatum, 61-62
conduct, 48, 53, 114
confidence, 74
consistency, 35
Constitution of Athens (Aristotle), 90
consubstantiation, 61
contention, 26
conversion, 89, 97
corruption, 82
Council of Trent, 14, 71
courage, 42
covenant, 86
Cranmer, Thomas, 86
Creed of Chalcedon, 59
crime, 82, 103
criticism, higher, viii; textual, viii, x, 25
crucifixion, 14, 65-66, 101
culture, ethical, 33

Damascus, 89
David, 88, 113
deacons, 1, 4
death, 11-12, 29, 31, 33, 35, 63-65, 72, 81, 85, 92; substitutionary, 40
Debrunner, A., 8, 50, 92
definition, 56-57
deism, 97
deity, 57
demons, 68
Demos, 11
Demosthenes, 46
depravity, 11; total, 16
depression, 116
destruction, 42, 101, 112
determinism, 74-75

Index

"Determinism and
  Responsibility" (Clark), 75
Dewey, John, 23-24
diakonoi, 3
dikaion, 17
discrimination, 22, 24
doctrine, 28, 40, 49, 53, 59, 91,
  113, 116, 119, 123
Doddridge, Philip, 71, 95
dogs, 85
dokimadzein, 22
dominion, 58
doulos, 2-3
duty, 71

Eadie, John, ix, 4, 6, 8, 11, 20,
  22, 27, 30-31, 35-39, 42, 47,
  49, 52, 70, 77, 81, 99, 104,
  106, 111-112, 114-117
Earth, 19, 30, 54, 68, 119
Edwards, Jonathan, 29; *Works*:
  "Sinners in the Hands of an
  Angry God," 29
efficiency, 24
Einstein, Albert, 112
eis, 7
election, 13-14, 16
Elijah, 102
Elizabeth, Queen, 86
Ellicott, Charles J., 21, 60, 63,
  71, 91, 94, 101, 109, 117
Emmaus, 105
emotion, 19-20, 47, 53, 106
en, 20-21, 38, 78
enmity, 112
enthymemes, 46
envy, 26
Epaphroditus, 80-83, 119
Ephesus, vii, 37, 109

Epicureans, 76, 101
Epicurus, 101
epignōsis, 20
episcopos, 3
*Epistle of Paul to the Philippians,
  The* (Martin), ix
essence, 55-57
Ethical Cultural Society, 32
ethics, 23, 50-52
Euodia, 107, 109
Euripides, 46
Eusebius, 67
Evangelical Quarterly, The, 75
evil, 50-51, 85, 122
exaltation, 67
excellence, 114
execution, 30, 32, 93
experience, 113

faith, 15, 23, 35, 39-40, 43, 70,
  73, 77-78, 85, 90-91, 98, 112
fear, 25, 70, 73-74, 123
feeling, 53
fellowship, 48
feminism, 109
flesh, 33-34, 62-63, 86-87
foolishness, 43
free will, 13-15, 71, 75
Freud, Sigmund, 20
fruit, 23, 33
fundamentalism, 40

Galatia, 27
Gamaliel, 88
Gentiles, 9, 41, 102, 121
Gingrich, F. W., 47, 72, 91, 98
glorification, 74
glory, 72, 102

gnōridzō, 34
gnōsis, 20
Gnostics, 104
God, 2, 4, 6, 11-12, 15-19, 24, 28, 34-35, 37, 41-43, 53, 55-57, 59-60, 66, 70-73, 75-76, 81, 90-91, 97-98, 100, 108, 111-113, 119-120, 123; the Father, 1, 15, 55, 58, 61, 68, 120; the Holy Spirit, 24, 30-31, 37-38, 45, 47-48, 71, 86-87, 100; law of, 49-50; mind of, 119; Son of, 53-55, 58, 64, 66, 112; wisdom of, 43; Word of, 13, 26
godliness, 123
Good News for Modern Man, viii
Gordon-Conwell Seminary, 32
Gospel, 2, 6-7, 9-11, 17-18, 25-27, 30-31, 34-36, 38-40, 48, 70, 77, 79, 85, 88, 91, 109, 115, 118, 121-122
gossip, 114
government, ecclesiastical, 3
grace, 1, 10, 12, 14-17, 29, 42, 67, 70, 73
grammar, 8, 18, 35, 43, 49, 103-104
gratitude, 74
Grayston, Kenneth, 1, 5, 17, 19, 32-33, 36, 52; *Works: Cambridge Bible Commentary on the New English Bible*, ix; *The Letter of Paul to the Philippians*, 54
Great Britain, 12, 36
Greek, ix
Gregory of Nyssa, 55-56
guidance, 24

happiness, 111
head, 20
headship, federal, 99, 114
heart, 17-18, 20, 43, 93, 114
Heaven, 12, 14, 16, 19, 28-29, 35, 58, 66, 69, 97, 102-104, 119-120
Hell, 16
Hendriksen, William, ix, 7-8, 10, 19, 22, 24, 30-31, 33-34, 40, 47, 49, 82, 91, 93-94, 96, 101, 103, 109, 111
Heraclitus, 116, 119
heresy, 26, 28
heroism, 103
Hesiod, 46
hina, 8
history, 112
Hocking, Ernest, 97
Hodge, Charles, 65; *Works: Systematic Theology*, 65
holiness, 12, 35, 58
Holland, 12
holy, 3
Homer, 46
homosexuals, 82
honesty, 114
Hort, F. J. A., viii, 87
hoti, 8
How Firm a Foundation, 13
Hume, David, 105
humiliation, 57, 61, 65-66, 102
Humiliation of Christ, The (Bruce), 65
humility, 50-51
hypostatical union, 65
hysteria, 116

ignorance, 22

immortality, 105
immutability, 13, 59
imputation, 91-92
ina, 46, 49-50
incarnation, 40, 58, 61-62, 64
incomprehensibility, 113
industry, 114
inerrancy, 40
inflation, 116
insincerity, 28
instruction, 123
intellect, 75, 99
intuition, 65
Ireland, 12
irrationalism, 113
Israel, 88, 113

James, 19
Jehovah, 101, 113
Jerome, 119
Jesus Christ, 1-2, 8-15, 18-19, 22-23, 25, 27-29, 31-36, 38, 42-43, 45-48, 52, 54-59, 61-63, 68, 76-79, 81-82, 85-86, 88-89, 90-97, 101-102, 104, 107, 110-111, 118-121; active and passive obedience of, 14; deity of, 59, 99; *see also* God
Jews, 41, 66, 85, 97, 121
John, 51
Judaizers, 27-28, 51, 85-88, 101-102
Judas Iscariot, 19, 28
judgment, 21-22, 24, 41, 90
Julius Caesar, 36
justice, 17
justification, 17, 23, 46, 74, 91

kenosis, 56-57, 59
kerygma, 40
Kierkegaard, Soren, 40
King James Version, vii-viii, 5, 15, 17, 21-22, 25, 29, 42, 49, 61, 68, 72, 83, 95, 118
knowledge, 20-21, 24, 49, 88-89, 93, 98, 114-115, 123
Knox, John, 74
Kohmeyer, 54
koinonia, 6-7, 47

Lamb's Book of Life, 108
Larger Catechism, 64
Latimer, Hugh, 31, 86
law, 21-22, 49, 86-89, 119; food, 27
Lazarus, 72, 104
Lenski, R. C. H., ix, 7-8, 10, 17-20, 30, 34-36, 39-40, 46, 48-49, 54, 62, 70, 76-78, 81, 84, 97, 101, 104, 113-115, 120
Letter of Paul to the Philippians, The (Grayston), 54
liberalism, 53, 96, 118, 122
licentiousness, 102
Liddell, Henry George, 72
life, 15, 29, 30-31, 33, 50, 52-53, 55, 69, 120,123; eternal, 15
Linguistic Key to the Greek New Testament (Rienecker), 57
linguistics, 17
lips, 20
liver, 19
logic, 60, 106, 119
logos, 55, 60, 62, 116-118
Lord, 1, 79-80, 84, 106, 111, 115, 123; *see also* God, Jesus Christ

Lord's Prayer, 97
love, 13, 16, 20-21, 27, 45, 47-49, 58
Lucian, 76
Luke, 79
Luther, Martin, 61, 66
Lutheran, 12, 61-62, 70, 73
Lydia, 107

Macedonia, 116, 118
manuscripts, ix
Mao, Chairman, 112
Martin, Ralph, 2, 5, 19, 23, 32, 34, 36, 52, 69, 79, 91, 98, 102, 109, 111-112, 114; *Works: The Epistle of Paul to the Philippians*, ix
Mary, 86, 104
mathematics, ix
Melanchthon, Phillip, 12, 62, 107
Mennonites, 103
merit, 11
message, 39
Messiah, 65, 89
metaphors, 78
Metzger, Bruce, 24, 52, 87; *Works: Textual Commentary*, 52
Meyer, H. A. W., 63, 90, 120
millennium, 120
mind, 2, 30-31, 41, 75, 93, 98, 113, 122
ministers, 122
miracles, 40-59, 85, 111
mneia, 5
modernists, 122; *see also* liberalism
morality, 53, 113
morphē, 55-57, 60, 65

Moses, 2-3, 102
motivation, 51
Motyer, J. A., 11, 19, 22, 36, 48, 53, 60, 67, 77, 81, 91, 111-112; *Works: Philippian Studies*, 4, 21
Moule, H. C. G., ix, 1, 18-19, 22, 27, 29-30, 104, 111
Muller, Jacobus J., ix, 5, 8-9, 19-20, 30, 36, 38, 47, 57, 59, 77, 79, 91, 93, 101, 107, 112, 117
murder, 51, 108
mutilation, 85
mysteries, 118

names, 107
nature, 55-56
Neander, 10
neo-orthodox, 122
Nero, 104
Nestlé, Erwin, 102, 114
Nestorianism, 56, 63-65
New American Standard Version, vii-viii, 21, 34, 41, 49, 72-73, 83
New English Bible, 5, 17, 33, 40, 46, 52, 63, 79
New International Version, vii-viii, 6, 21, 29, 33, 38, 40, 49, 52, 68, 72, 80, 83, 87, 107, 115
New Testament, vii-ix, 2, 5, 54, 56, 58, 77-78, 93-94, 96, 109, 114, 118
Nicene Creed, 117
Noe, 9
Northern Ireland, 108

oath, 19
obedience, 21, 49
observation, 11
Old Testament, viii, 2, 66, 76, 89, 93, 97, 119
omnipotence, 66, 71, 75; see God
omnipresence, 61, 110; see God
omniscience, 58, 71; see God
organization, para-church, 53
orthodoxy, 122
Outline of Lectures in Systematic Theology, An (Thiessen), 58
overseer, 3

pagans, 42
Paraclete, 47
paradox, 113
paramenō, 35-36
Park Street Church, 32
parousia, 36
pastors, 4
Paul, vii-x, 1-2, 4-7, 9, 11, 17-20, 22, 25-26, 28-37, 39-40, 42-45, 48-51, 53-54, 56, 62, 69, 71, 73-87, 89, 92-97, 100-101, 108, 111, 115, 118, 121
Paul of Samosata, 67
peace, 1, 111, 113
Pelagius, 71, 117
Pennsylvania, University of, 29
Pentecostalists, 100
perception, 21
perfection, 15, 96-97
persecution, 43, 71, 82, 109-110
perseverance, 11, 16
person, 55
Peter, 44, 71, 85
petitions, 6

Pharisees, 63, 66, 88-89
Philippi, vii, ix, 1, 3, 37-38, 41, 80-82, 99, 106, 108-109
Philippian Studies (Motyer), 4, 21
Philippians (Tenney), ix
Philo of Alexandria, 119
phronetē, 49
phusis, 65
Physics (Aristotle), ix
physiology, 19
pietism, 32
pisteuō, 39
pistis, 39
Plato, 19, 46, 105, 117; *Works: Apology*, 91; *Timaeus*, ix
pleasure, 33, 116
pneuma, 39
pneumati, 38
poetry, 54
polemics, 85
Polycarp, 31, 84
polytheism, 116
pope, 86
practical, 53
Praetorian Guard, 25
Praetorium, 25-26
praise, 114
prayer, 5, 31, 110
preachers, 27, 32, 85
preaching, 26-28, 30-31, 37, 40
predestination, 71
Predestination (Clark), 72
Predestination in the Old Testament (Clark), 72
Presbyterians, 12
pride, 50, 73
prophets, 2; false, 51
providence, 44
psūche, 39

psychology, 19, 26, 28
punctuation, 90
punishment, 15, 66, 73
purgatory, 35
Puritans, 12, 29

reason, 46, 80, 84, 119
Reformation, 12, 14
regeneration, 11, 69-71, 73-74, 112; baptismal, 86
religions, mystery, 117
repentance, 53
reprobate, 68, 94
reprobation, 70
responsibility, 74-75
resurrection, 12, 67, 81, 92-94, 97, 104; bodily, 40
revelation, 11, 35, 80, 100, 111
reverence, 73-74
Revised Standard Version, viii, 5-6, 9, 17, 21, 33, 49, 52, 61, 63, 68, 72-73, 80, 87, 107, 115
Ridley, Nicholas, 31, 86
Rienecker, Fritz, 58; *Works: Linguistic Key to the Greek New Testament*, 57
righteousness, 17, 23, 53, 90-92
Rock of Ages (Toplady), 41
Roman Catholicism, 3, 14, 86
Roman Emperor, 104
Rome, 26, 38, 80-81, 121

sacrifice, 73, 77-78
Sadducees, 28
saints, 1-3, 11, 16, 86, 121; perseverance of, 10, 13, 17, 40
salvation, 10, 15-16, 27-31, 41-42, 68-71, 74, 88, 123

sanctification, 3, 23, 48, 69, 74, 97, 99, 120, 123
Sanhedrin, 108
sarcasm, 85
Satan, 15, 68, 71
Saturn, viii-ix
Saul, King, 88
savior, 104
Schleiermacher, Friedrich, 107
scholarship, viii
schools, public, 90, 103
Scott, E. F., 32, 72
Scripture, 15, 59, 62, 100, 104, 113, 123; *see also* Bible
second coming of Christ, 109
security, eternal, 13, 69; *see also* saints, perseverance of
self-sufficiency, 117
Sennacherib, 112
sensation, 20-22
sentimentality, viii
serenity, 111
sexual intercourse, 93
Shedd, W. G. T., 55
Shorter Catechism, 12, 24
sign, 43
Silas, 108
sin, 11, 22, 51, 67, 72-73, 111
"Sinners in the Hands of an Angry God" (Edwards), 29
slavery, 2
Socrates, 35
sorites, 46
soteriology, 58
soul-sleep, 35
sovereignty, 71, 74; *see also* omnipotence
Spain, 36
spirit, 121
splagchnois, 19

Stephen, 28
Stoicism, 119
Stoics, 116-117, 119
strife, 50-51
style, vii
subsistence, 55
substance, 55-56, 65
suffering, 44, 66
suicide, 24, 33, 57, 103, 116
Switzerland, 12
Syntyche, 107, 109
system, 16
Systematic Theology (Hodge), 65

Tarsus, 88
Taylor, Jeremy, 117
teachers, false, 71, 107, 109
teaching, Pauline, 99
temptation, 15, 71
Ten Commandments, 3
Tenney, Merrill C., ix, 19, 27, 36; *Works: Philippians*, ix
Tertullian, 116-117
Textual Commentary (Metzger), 52
Textus Receptus, 42, 52, 73, 118
thanksgiving, 5-6
theism, 97
theology, 7, 39, 41, 53, 118, 122
theoretical, 53
Thessalonica, 118
Thiessen, Henry C., 58; *Works: An Outline of Lectures in Systematic Theology*, 58
thinking, 45, 53
thrift, 114
Timaeus (Plato), ix
Timothy, 1-2, 78-81, 107
Tischendorf, 42, 90, 102

Toplady, Augustus, 41; *Works: Rock of Ages*, 41
transcendence, 3
translation, vii, 72-73, 78, 95
De Trinitate (Augustine), 55
Trinity, 55-56, 59, 87, 113-114, 116, 119
truth, 17, 21-22, 27, 39-40, 53, 58-59, 99, 113, 123
TULIP, 40

ubiquity, 61
understanding, 21, 112, 123
U.S. Navy, 3
uper, 73

value, 24
vanity, 50-51
Vaticanus, 90
verbum, 119
virgin birth, 85
virtue, 114, 116
volition, 20

Wesley, John, 71
Wesleyanism, 97
Westcott, B. F., viii, 87
Westminster Confession, 10, 12, 59, 64, 74
What Do Presbyterians Believe? (Clark), 12
Wikgren, Allen, 87
will, 56
wisdom, 120, 123
Word of God, 14; *see also* Bible, Jesus Christ, Scripture
works, 23, 70, 73, 86, 88, 123

worship, 86

Xenophon, 46

Yorick, 104

Zechariah, 102
Zwingli, Ulrich, 62

Scripture Index

Acts	ix
1:2	9
1:18	19
2:29	9
3:21	9
5:41	44
6:9-10	28
7:18	9
9:29	28
16:12-40	41
20	37
20:25	37
22:1	28
23:1	9

Colossians	2
1:24	44, 93
2:2	21
2:9	59
3:22	2

1 Corinthians	
1:10	41
1:24-25	43
2:6	98
4:6	73
4:16	100
6:13	105
7:2ff	2
9:3	28
10:30	73
11:1	100
11:2	77
14:20	98
15	105
15:2	77

2 Corinthians	viii
3:1-4:6	90
4:5,6	43
6:10	77
7:11	28
8:1-2	116
10:13,14	9
11:23-28	120

Deuteronomy	
32:5	76

Ecclesiastes	
7:20	97

Ephesians	
1:16	5
2:8	43
4:13	98

Galatians	viii, 23, 109
5:3,4	86

Hebrews	1
1:3	59
5:1	72
5:14	21
12:28	74

Isaiah	
29:13	20

45:9	74	**Luke**	
55:11	15	1:20	9
64:8	74	2:52	64
		9:45	21
James		9:50	73
2:1	39	12:19	65
3:2-4	97	17:27	9
4:13-15	78	20:35	94
Jeremiah		**Mark**	
18:6	74	9:10	28
31:3	15	12:28	28
32:40	15, 74		
		Matthew	
Job		6:12	96
13:16	30	6:25	110
		8:27	43
John	2	24:38	9
1:1	116, 118-119	24:47	91
1:9	59	26:38	64
2:18	43		
2:24, 25	59	**1 Peter**	
4:23	86	1:5	15, 39
10:28-29	15	1:7, 9	39
11:4	72	1:17	74
		3:15	28
1 John		4:9	76
1:8	97		
1:9	50	**2 Peter**	
2:5	21	1:1	39, 79
2:19	15		
5:2, 3	21	**Philippians**	
5:4	39	1:3-7	4
		1:4, 5	7
Jude		1:6	15, 73
3	39	1:7	28, 98
20	39	1:8-11	19
		1:13	26
1 Kings		1:18	30
8:46	97	1:19	30

Scripture Index

1:27, 30	84	8:3	62
1:28	69	9:21-24	74
2:12	10	13:10	21
2:13	11	15:24, 28	36
2:17, 23, 24	37		
3:9	92	**2 Samuel**	
3:15	20, 98	17:14	75
4:2	50		
4:8, 9	22	**1 Thessalonians**	2
4:16	7	1:2	5
		4:16	94
Philemon	2	5:21	77
10, 13, 22	37		
		2 Thessalonians	2
Proverbs		3:17	1
23:17	73		
28:4	73	**1 Timothy**	
		1:2, 4, 19	39
Psalms		1:4, 9	85
78:8	76	1:8	87
		2:7, 9, 13	39
Revelation	54	3:14	2
1:1	2	4:1, 6	39
2:13	39	5:8, 12	39
2:20	2	6:10, 12, 21	39
7:3	2		
10:7	2	**2 Timothy**	
11:18	2	1:6	2
14:12	39	2:19	15
15:3	3	3:6	5
19:2, 5	3	3:8	39
20:5	94	4:7	39
22:3, 6	3	4:16	79
Romans		**Titus**	
1	viii	1:4, 13	39
1:9	5	2:2	39
1:28	21	2:14	85
3:1	87	3:9	85
6:16ff	2	3:15	39
7:14-24	97		

THE CRISIS OF OUR TIME

Historians have christened the thirteenth century the Age of Faith and termed the eighteenth century the Age of Reason. The twentieth century has been called many things: the Atomic Age, the Age of Inflation, the Age of the Tyrant, the Age of Aquarius. But it deserves one name more than the others: the Age of Irrationalism. Contemporary secular intellectuals are anti-intellectual. Contemporary philosophers are anti-philosophy. Contemporary theologians are anti-theology.

In past centuries, secular philosophers have generally believed that knowledge is possible to man. Consequently they expended a great deal of thought and effort trying to justify knowledge. In the twentieth century, however, the optimism of the secular philosophers has all but disappeared. They despair of knowledge.

Like their secular counterparts, the great theologians and doctors of the church taught that knowledge is possible to man. Yet the theologians of the twentieth century have repudiated that belief. They also despair of knowledge. This radical skepticism has filtered down from the philosophers and theologians and penetrated our entire culture, from television to music to literature. *The Christian in the twentieth century is confronted with an overwhelming cultural consensus—sometimes stated explicitly but most often implicitly: Man does not and cannot know anything truly.*

What does this have to do with Christianity? Simply this: If man can know nothing truly, man can truly know nothing. We cannot know that the Bible is the Word of God, that Christ died for his people, or that Christ is alive today at the right hand of the Father. Unless knowledge is possible, Christianity is nonsensical, for it claims to be knowledge. What is at stake in the twentieth century is not simply a single doctrine, such as the virgin birth, or the existence of Hell, as important as those doctrines may be, but the whole of Christianity itself. If knowledge is not possible to man, it is worse than silly to argue points of doctrine–it is insane.

The irrationalism of the present age is so thoroughgoing and pervasive that even the Remnant–the segment of the professing church that remains faithful–has accepted much of it, frequently without even being aware of what it was accepting. In some circles this irrationalism has become synonymous with piety and humility, and those who oppose it are denounced as rationalists–as though to be logical were a sin. Our contemporary anti-theologians make a contradiction and call it a Mystery. The faithful ask for truth and are given Paradox. If any balk at swallowing the absurdities of the anti-theologians, they are frequently marked as heretics or schismatics who seek to act independently of God.

There is no greater threat facing the true church of Christ at this moment than the irrationalism that now controls our entire culture. Totalitarianism, guilty of tens of millions of murders–including those of millions of Christians–is to be feared, but not nearly so much as the idea that we do not and cannot know the truth. Hedonism, the popular philosophy of America, is not to be feared so much as the belief that logic–that "mere human logic," to use the religious irrationalists' own phrase–is futile. The attacks on truth, on revelation, on the intellect, and on logic are renewed daily. But note well: The misologists–the haters of logic–use logic to demonstrate the futility of using logic. The anti-intellectuals construct intricate intellectual arguments to prove the insufficiency of the intellect. The anti-theologians use the revealed Word of God to show that there can be no revealed Word of God–or that if there could, it would remain impenetrable darkness and Mystery to our finite minds.

Nonsense Has Come

Is it any wonder that the world is grasping at straws–the straws of experientialism, mysticism, and drugs? After all, if people are told that the Bible contains insoluble mysteries, then is not a flight into mysticism to be expected? On what grounds can it be condemned? Certainly not on logical grounds or Biblical grounds, if logic is futile and the Bible unintelligible. Moreover, if it cannot be condemned on logical or Biblical grounds, it cannot be condemned at all. If people are going to have a religion of the mysterious, they will not adopt Christianity: They will have a genuine mystery religion. "Those who call for Nonsense," C.S. Lewis once wrote, "will find that it comes." And that is precisely what

The Crisis of Our Time

has happened. The popularity of Eastern mysticism, of drugs, and of religious experience is the logical consequence of the irrationalism of the twentieth century. There can and will be no Christian reformation–and no reconstruction of society–unless and until the irrationalism of the age is totally repudiated by Christians.

The Church Defenseless

Yet how shall they do it? The spokesmen for Christianity have been fatally infected with irrationalism. The seminaries, which annually train thousands of men to teach millions of Christians, are the finishing schools of irrationalism, completing the job begun by the government schools and colleges. Some of the pulpits of the most conservative churches (we are not speaking of the apostate churches) are occupied by graduates of the anti-theological schools. These products of modern anti-theological education, when asked to give a reason for the hope that is in them, can generally respond with only the intellectual analogue of a shrug–a mumble about Mystery. They have not grasped–and therefore cannot teach those for whom they are responsible–the first truth: "And you shall know the truth." Many, in fact, explicitly deny it, saying that, at best, we possess only "pointers" to the truth, or something "similar" to the truth, a mere analogy. Is the impotence of the Christian church a puzzle? Is the fascination with pentecostalism and faith healing among members of conservative churches an enigma? Not when one understands the sort of studied nonsense that is purveyed in the name of God in the seminaries.

The Trinity Foundation

The creators of The Trinity Foundation firmly believe that theology is too important to be left to the licensed theologians–the graduates of the schools of theology. They have created The Trinity Foundation for the express purpose of teaching the faithful all that the Scriptures contain–not warmed over, baptized, secular philosophies. Each member of the board of directors of The Trinity Foundation has signed this oath: "I believe that the Bible alone and the Bible in its entirety is the Word of God and, therefore, inerrant in the autographs. I believe that the system of truth presented in the Bible is best summarized in the Westminster Confession of Faith. So help me God."

The ministry of The Trinity Foundation is the presentation of the system of truth taught in Scripture as clearly and as completely as possible. We do not regard obscurity as a virtue, nor confusion as a sign of spirituality. Confusion, like all error, is sin, and teaching that confusion is all that Christians can hope for is doubly sin.

The presentation of the truth of Scripture necessarily involves the rejection of error. The Foundation has exposed and will continue to expose the irrationalism of the twentieth century, whether its current spokesman be an existentialist philosopher or a professed Reformed theologian. We oppose anti-intellectualism, whether it be espoused by a neo-orthodox theologian or a fundamentalist evangelist. We reject misology, whether it be on the lips of a neo-evangelical or those of a Roman Catholic charismatic. To each error we bring the brilliant light of Scripture, proving all things, and holding fast to that which is true.

The Primacy of Theory

The ministry of The Trinity Foundation is not a "practical" ministry. If you are a pastor, we will not enlighten you on how to organize an ecumenical prayer meeting in your community or how to double church attendance in a year. If you are a homemaker, you will have to read elsewhere to find out how to become a total woman. If you are a businessman, we will not tell you how to develop a social conscience. The professing church is drowning in such "practical" advice.

The Trinity Foundation is unapologetically theoretical in its outlook, believing that theory without practice is dead, and that practice without theory is blind. The trouble with the professing church is not primarily in its practice, but in its theory. Christians do not know, and many do not even care to know, the doctrines of Scripture. Doctrine is intellectual, and Christians are generally anti-intellectual. Doctrine is ivory tower philosophy, and they scorn ivory towers. The ivory tower, however, is the control tower of a civilization. It is a fundamental, theoretical mistake of the practical men to think that they can be merely practical, for practice is always the practice of some theory. The relationship between theory and practice is the relationship between cause and effect. If a person believes correct theory, his practice will tend to be correct. The practice of contemporary Christians is immoral because it is the practice of false theories. It is a major theoretical mistake of the practical men to think that they can ignore the ivory towers of the philosophers and theologians as irrelevant to their lives. Every action that the "practical" men take is governed by the thinking that has occurred in some ivory tower-whether that tower be the British Museum; the Academy; a home in Basel, Switzerland; or a tent in Israel.

In Understanding Be Men

It is the first duty of the Christian to understand correct theory-correct doctrine-and thereby implement correct practice. This order-first theory, then practice-is both logical and Biblical. It is, for example, exhibited in Paul's epistle to the Romans, in which he spends the first eleven chapters expounding theory and the last five discussing practice. The contemporary teachers of Christians have not only reversed the order, they have inverted the Pauline emphasis on theory and practice. The virtually complete failure of the teachers of the professing church to instruct the faithful in correct doctrine is the cause of the misconduct and cultural impotence of Christians. The church's lack of power is the result of its lack of truth. The *Gospel* is the power of God, not religious experience or personal relationship. The church has no power because it has abandoned the Gospel, the good news, for a religion of experientialism. Twentieth-century American Christians are children carried about by every wind of doctrine, not knowing what they believe, or even if they believe anything for certain.

The chief purpose of The Trinity Foundation is to counteract the irrationalism of the age and to expose the errors of the teachers of the church. Our emphasis-on the Bible as the sole source of truth, on the primacy of the intellect, on the supreme importance of correct doctrine, and on the necessity for systematic and logical thinking-is almost unique in Christendom. To the extent that the church survives-and she will survive and flourish-it will be because of her increasing acceptance of these basic ideas and their logical implications.

We believe that the Trinity Foundation is filling a vacuum in Christendom. We are saying that Christianity is intellectually defensible-that, in fact, it is the only intellectually defensible system of thought. We are saying that God has made the wisdom of this world-whether that wisdom be called science, religion, philosophy, or common sense-foolishness. We are appealing to all Christians who have not conceded defeat in the intellectual battle with the world to join us in our efforts to raise a standard to which all men of sound mind can repair.

The love of truth, of God's Word, has all but disappeared in our time.

We are committed to and pray for a great instauration. But though we may not see this reformation of Christendom in our lifetimes, we believe it is our duty to present the whole counsel of God because Christ has commanded it. The results of our teaching are in God's hands, not ours. Whatever those results, his Word is never taught in vain, but always accomplishes the result that he intended it to accomplish. Professor Gordon H. Clark has stated our view well:

> There have been times in the history of God's people, for example, in the days of Jeremiah, when refreshing grace and widespread revival were not to be expected: The time was one of chastisement. If this twentieth century is of a similar nature, individual Christians here and there can find comfort and strength in a study of God's Word. But if God has decreed happier days for us and if we may expect a world-shaking and genuine spiritual awakening, then it is the author's belief that a zeal for souls, however necessary, is not the sufficient condition. Have there not been devout saints in every age, numerous enough to carry on a revival? Twelve such persons are plenty. What distinguishes the arid ages from the period of the Reformation, when nations were moved as they had not been since Paul preached in Ephesus, Corinth, and Rome, is the latter's fullness of knowledge of God's Word. To echo an early Reformation thought, when the ploughman and the garage attendant know the Bible as well as the theologian does, and know it better than some contemporary theologians, then the desired awakening shall have already occurred.

In addition to publishing books, the Foundation publishes a monthly newsletter, *The Trinity Review*. Subscriptions to *The Review* are free to U.S. addresses; please write to the address below to become a subscriber. If you would like further information or would like to join us in our work, please let us know.

The Trinity Foundation is a non-profit foundation, tax exempt under section 501 (c)(3) of the Internal Revenue Code of 1954. You can help us disseminate the Word of God through your tax-deductible contributions to the Foundation.

John W. Robbins

INTELLECTUAL AMMUNITION

The Trinity Foundation is committed to the reformation of philosophy and theology along Biblical lines. We regard God's command to bring all our thoughts into conformity with Christ very seriously, and the books listed below are designed to accomplish that goal. They are written with two subordinate purposes: (1) to demolish all secular claims to knowledge; and (2) to build a system of truth based upon the Bible alone.

Philosophy

Behaviorism and Christianity, Gordon H. Clark $6.95
  Behaviorism *is a critique of both secular and religious behaviorists. It includes chapters on John Watson, Edgar S. Singer, Jr., Gilbert Ryle, B.F. Skinner, and Donald MacKay. Clark's refutation of behaviorism and his argument for a Christian doctrine of man are unanswerable.*

A Christian Philosophy of Education $8.95
Gordon H. Clark
  The first edition of this book was published in 1946. It sparked the contemporary interest in Christian schools. Dr. Clark thoroughly revised and updated it, and it is needed now more than ever. Its chapters include: The Need for a World-View, The Christian World-View, The Alternative to Christian Theism, Neutrality, Ethics, The Christian Philosophy of Education, Academic Matters, Kindergarten to University. Three appendices are included as well: The Relationship of Public Education to Christianity, A Protestant World-View, and Art and the Gospel.

A Christian View of Men and Things $10.95
Gordon H. Clark
  No other book achieves what A Christian View *does: the presentation of Christianity as it applies to history, politics, ethics, science, religion, and epistemology. Clark's command of both worldly philosophy and*

Scripture is evident on every page, and the result is a breathtaking and invigorating challenge to the wisdom of this world.

Clark Speaks From The Grave, Gordon H. Clark $3.95
Dr. Clark chides some of his critics for their failure to defend Christianity competently. Clark Speaks is a stimulating and illuminating discussion of the errors of contemporary apologists.

Education, Christianity, and the State $9.95
J. Gresham Machen
Machen was one of the foremost educators, theologians, and defenders of Christianity in the twentieth century. The author of numerous scholarly books, Machen saw clearly that if Christianity is to survive and flourish, a system of Christian schools must be established. This collection of essays captures his thoughts on education over nearly three decades.

Essays on Ethics and Politics, Gordon H. Clark $10.95
Clark's essays, written over the course of five decades, are a major statement of Christian ethics.

Gordon H. Clark: Personal Recollections $6.95
John W. Robbins, editor
Friends of Dr. Clark have written their recollections of the man. Contributors include family members, colleagues, students, and friends such as Harold Lindsell, Carl Henry, Ronald Nash, Dwight Zeller, and Mary Crumpacker. The book includes an extensive bibliography of Clark's work.

Historiography: Secular and Religious $13.95
Gordon H. Clark
In this masterful work, Clark applies his philosophy to the writing of history, examining all the major schools of historiography.

An Introduction to Christian Philosophy $8.95
Gordon H. Clark
In 1966 Clark delivered three lectures on philosophy at Wheaton College. In these lectures he criticizes secular philosophy and launches a

philosophical revolution in the name of Christ.

Language and Theology, Gordon H. Clark $9.95
There are two main currents in twentieth-century philosophy–language philosophy and existentialism. Both are hostile to Christianity. Clark disposes of language philosophy in this brilliant critique of Bertrand Russell, Ludwig Wittgenstein, Rudolf Carnap, A.J. Ayer, Langdon Gilkey, and many others.

Logic, Gordon H. Clark $8.95
Written as a textbook for Christian schools, Logic *is another unique book from Clark's pen. His presentation of the laws of thought, which must be followed if Scripture is to be understood correctly, and which are found in Scripture itself, is both clear and thorough.* Logic *is an indispensable book for the thinking Christian.*

Logic Workbook, Elihu Carranza $11.95
Designed to be used in conjunction with Clark's textbook Logic, *this* Workbook *contains hundreds of exercises and test questions on perforated pages for ease of use by students.*

Logic Workbook Answer Key, Elihu Carranza $2.95
The Key *contains answers to all the exercises and tests in the* Workbook.

Lord God of Truth, Concerning the Teacher $7.95
Gordon H. Clark and Aurelius Augustine
This essay by Clark summarizes many of the most telling arguments against empiricism and defends the Biblical teaching that we know God and truth immediately. The dialogue by Augustine is a refutation of empirical language philosophy.

The Philosophy of Science and Belief in God $8.95
Gordon H. Clark
In opposing the contemporary idolatry of science, Clark analyzes three major aspects of science: the problem of motion, Newtonian science, and modern theories of physics. His conclusion is that science, while it may be useful, is always false; and he demonstrates its falsity in numer-

ous ways. Since science is always false, it can offer no objection to the Bible and Christianity.

Religion, Reason and Revelation $10.95
Gordon H. Clark
One of Clark's apologetical masterpieces, Religion, Reason and Revelation has been praised for the clarity of its thought and language. It includes chapters on Is Christianity a Religion? Faith and Reason, Inspiration and Language, Revelation and Morality, and God and Evil. It is must reading for all serious Christians.

Thales to Dewey: A History of Philosophy paper $13.95
Gordon H. Clark hardback $18.95
This is the best one-volume history of philosophy in English.

Three Types of Religious Philosophy $6.95
Gordon H. Clark
In this book on apologetics, Clark examines empiricism, rationalism, dogmatism, and contemporary irrationalism, which does not rise to the level of philosophy. He offers a solution to the question, "How can Christianity be defended before the world?"

William James and John Dewey $8.95
Gordon H. Clark
William James and John Dewey are two of the most influential philosophers America has produced. Their philosophies of instrumentalism and pragmatism are hostile to Christianity, and Clark demolishes their arguments.

Theology

The Atonement, Gordon H. Clark $8.95
In The Atonement, *Clark discusses the covenants, the virgin birth and incarnation, federal headship and representation, the relationship between God's sovereignty and justice, and much more. He analyzes traditional views of the atonement and criticizes them in the light of Scripture alone.*

Intellectual Ammunition 149

The Biblical Doctrine of Man, Gordon H. Clark $6.95
Is man soul and body or soul, spirit, and body? What is the image of God? Is Adam's sin imputed to his children? Is evolution true? Are men totally depraved? What is the heart? These are some of the questions discussed and answered from Scripture in this book.

The Clark–Van Til Controversy $7.95
Herman Hoeksema
This collection of essays by the founder of the Protestant Reformed Church–essays written at the time of the Clark–Van Til controversy–is one of the best commentaries on the events in print.

Cornelius Van Til: The Man and The Myth $2.45
John W. Robbins
The actual teachings of this eminent Philadelphia theologian have been obscured by the myths that surround him. This book penetrates those myths and criticizes Van Til's surprisingly unorthodox views of God and the Bible.

The Everlasting Righteousness, Horatius Bonar $8.95
Originally published in 1874, the language of Bonar's masterpiece on justification by faith alone has been updated and Americanized for easy reading and clear understanding. This is one of the best books ever written on justification.

Faith and Saving Faith, Gordon H. Clark $6.95
The views of the Roman Catholic church, John Calvin, Thomas Manton, John Owen, Charles Hodge, and B.B. Warfield are discussed in this book. Is the object of faith a person or a proposition? Is faith more than belief? Is belief more than thinking with assent, as Augustine said? In a world chaotic with differing views of faith, Clark clearly explains the Biblical view of faith and saving faith.

God and Evil, Gordon H. Clark $4.95
This volume is Chapter 5 of Religion, Reason and Revelation, in which Clark presents his solution to the problem of evil.

God's Hammer: The Bible and Its Critics $10.95
Gordon H. Clark
The starting point of Christianity, the doctrine on which all other doc-

trines depend, is "The Bible alone, and the Bible in its entirety, is the Word of God written, and therefore inerrant in the autographs." Over the centuries the opponents of Christianity, with Satanic shrewdness, have concentrated their attacks on the truthfulness and completeness of the Bible. In the twentieth century the attack is not so much in the fields of history and archaeology as in philosophy. Clark's brilliant defense of the complete truthfulness of the Bible is captured in this collection of eleven major essays.

Guide to the Westminster Confession and Catechism
James E. Bordwine $13.95

This large book contains the full text of both the Westminster Confession (both original and American versions) and the Larger Catechism. In addition, it offers a chapter-by-chapter summary of the Confession and a unique index to both the Confession and the Catechism.

The Holy Spirit, Gordon H. Clark $8.95

This discussion of the third person of the Trinity is both concise and exact. Clark includes chapters on the work of the Spirit, sanctification, and Pentecostalism. This book is part of his multi-volume systematic theology that began appearing in print in 1985.

The Incarnation, Gordon H. Clark $8.95

Who is Christ? The attack on the incarnation in the nineteenth and twentieth centuries has been vigorous, but the orthodox response has been lame. Clark reconstructs the doctrine of the incarnation, building and improving upon the Chalcedonian definition.

In Defense of Theology, Gordon H. Clark $9.95

There are four groups to whom Clark addresses this book: average Christians who are uninterested in theology, atheists and agnostics, religious experientialists, and serious Christians. The vindication of the knowledge of God against the objections of three of these groups is the first step in theology.

The Johannine Logos, Gordon H. Clark $5.95

Clark analyzes the relationship between Christ, who is the truth, and the Bible. He explains why John used the same word to refer to both Christ and his teaching. Chapters deal with the Prologue to John's

Gospel, Logos and Rheemata, Truth, and Saving Faith.

Justification by Faith Alone, Charles Hodge $10.95
Charles Hodge of Princeton Seminary was the best American theologian of the nineteenth century. Here in one volume are his two major essays on justification. This book is essential in defending the faith.

Predestination, Gordon H. Clark $8.95
Clark thoroughly discusses one of the most controversial and pervasive doctrines of the Bible: that God is, quite literally, Almighty. Free will, the origin of evil, God's omniscience, creation, and the new birth are all presented within a Scriptural framework. The objections of those who do not believe in the Almighty God are considered and refuted. This edition also contains the text of the booklet, Predestination in the Old Testament.

Sanctification, Gordon H. Clark $8.95
In this book, which is part of Clark's multi-volume systematic theology, he discusses historical theories of sanctification, the sacraments, and the Biblical doctrine of sanctification.

Study Guide to the Westminster Confession $10.95
W. Gary Crampton
This Study Guide *may be used by individuals or classes. It contains a paragraph by paragraph summary of the Westminster Confession, and questions for the student to answer. Space for answers is provided. The* Guide *will be most beneficial when used in conjunction with Clark's* What Do Presbyterians Believe?

Today's Evangelism: Counterfeit or Genuine? $6.95
Gordon H. Clark
Clark compares the methods and messages of today's evangelists with Scripture, and finds that Christianity is on the wane because the Gospel has been distorted or lost. This is an extremely useful and enlightening book.

The Trinity, Gordon H. Clark $8.95
Apart from the doctrine of Scripture, no teaching of the Bible is more

152   Philippians

important than the doctrine of God. Clark's defense of the orthodox doctrine of the Trinity is a principal portion of Clark's systematic theology. There are chapters on the deity of Christ, Augustine, the incomprehensibility of God, Bavinck and Van Til, and the Holy Spirit, among others.

What Calvin Says, W. Gary Crampton $7.95
   This is both a readable and thorough introduction to the theology of John Calvin.

What Do Presbyterians Believe? Gordon H. Clark $8.95
   This classic introduction to Christian doctrine has been republished. It is the best commentary on the Westminster Confession of Faith that has ever been written. A Study Guide *is now available for it.*

Commentaries on the New Testament

Colossians, Gordon H. Clark	$ 6.95
Ephesians, Gordon H. Clark	$ 8.95
First Corinthians, Gordon H. Clark	$10.95
First John, Gordon H. Clark	$10.95
First and Second Thessalonians, Gordon H. Clark	$ 5.95
New Heavens, New Earth (First and Second Peter) Gordon H. Clark	$10.95
The Pastoral Epistles (I and II Timothy and Titus) Gordon H. Clark	$ 9.95
Philippians, Gordon H. Clark	$ 9.95

All of Clark's commentaries are expository, not technical, and are written for the Christian layman. His purpose is to explain the text clearly and accurately so that the Word of God will be thoroughly known by every Christian.

The Trinity Library

We will send you one copy of each of the 48 books listed above for $310. You may also order the books you want individually on the order blank on the next page. Because some of the books are in short supply, we must reserve the right to substitute others of equal or greater value in The Trinity Library. This special offer expires June 30, 2000.

Order Form

Name _____

Address _____

_____

Please: ☐ add my name to the mailing list for *The Trinity Review*. I understand that there is no charge for the *Review* sent to a U.S. address.

☐ accept my tax deductible contribution of $_____ for the work of the Foundation.

☐ send me _____ copies of *Philippians*. I enclose as payment $_____.

☐ send me the Trinity Library of 48 books. I enclose US$310 as full payment.

☐ send me the following books. I enclose full payment in the amount of $ _____ for them.

_____
_____
_____
_____
_____

Mail to:
The Trinity Foundation
Post Office Box 1666, Hobbs, New Mexico 88240
United States of America

Please add $1.00 for postage on orders less than $10. For foreign orders, please enclose 20 percent of the total value of the books ordered. Thank you. For quantity discounts, please write to the Foundation.